Costing

Tutorial

AAT Diploma Pathway Unit 6

David Cox

osborne
BOOKS

Published by Osborne Books Limited
Unit 1B Everoak Estate
Bromyard Road
Worcester WR2 5HP
Tel 01905 748071
Email books@osbornebooks.co.uk
Website www.osbornebooks.co.uk

Design by Richard Holt
Cover image from Getty Images

Printed by the Bath Press, Bath

British Library Cataloguing in Publication Data
A catalogue record for this book is available from the British Library

ISBN 1 905777 05 1

Contents

Introduction

Acknowledgements

The publisher wishes to thank the following for their help with the reading and production of the book: Jean Cox, Michael Gilbert, Claire McCarthy and Liz Smith. Thanks are also due to Richard Holt for his designs for this new series.

The publisher is indebted to the Association of Accounting Technicians for its generous help and advice to our author and editors during the preparation of this text, and for permission to reproduce extracts from the AAT Unit Specification.

The development of the content of this book would not have been possible without the help and advice of a number of practising AAT lecturers. In particular the editorial team would like to thank Claire Eccleston of Hereford College of Technology and Kevin Fisher of Gloucester College of Arts and Technology for their useful suggestions and practical contributions.

Lastly, the publisher would pass special thanks to Roger Petheram, who as main consultant for this text and an experienced accounting lecturer at Worcester College of Technology, has provided invaluable help in reading, checking and providing practical advice in the writing and production process.

Author

David Cox has more than twenty years' experience teaching accountancy students over a wide range of levels. Formerly with the Management and Professional Studies Department at Worcester College of Technology, he now lectures on a freelance basis and carries out educational consultancy work in accountancy studies. He is author and joint author of a number of textbooks in the areas of accounting, finance and banking.

Introduction

Osborne tutorials

Costing Tutorial has been written to provide a study resource for students taking courses based on the AAT Diploma Pathway Unit 6 'Recording and analysing costs and revenues'.

Costing Tutorial deals with the recording and analysis of direct and indirect costs, including the allocation, apportionment and absorption of overhead costs. An important aspect is the use of costing information to help with decision-making – in the short-term and long-term.

The chapters of *Costing Tutorial* contain:

- a clear text with worked examples and case studies
- a chapter summary and key terms to help with revision
- student activities – with answers at the end of the book

The tutorial text – with questions and answers – is therefore useful for classroom use and also for distance learning students.

Osborne Workbooks

Costing Workbook, which accompanies this tutorial text, contains extended student activities, and practice Examinations. If you would like the *Costing Workbook*, please telephone the Osborne Books Sales Office on 01905 748071 for details of mail ordering, or visit the 24-hour online shop at www.osbornebooks.co.uk

Osborne Tutor Packs

The answers to the Activities and Examination tasks in the *Workbook* are available in a separate *Tutor Pack*. Contact the Osborne Books Sales Office on 01905 748071 or visit the website for details of how to obtain the Tutor Pack.

surfing with www.osbornebooks.co.uk

The Osborne Books website is constantly developing its range of facilities for tutors and students. Popular features include free downloadable resources and the on-line shop. Log on and try us!

1 An introduction to cost accounting

- the purpose of cost accounting and its role in providing information to the managers of a business
- cost units and cost centres
- identification and coding of costs and revenues
- the categories into which costs can be classified
  - by element
  - by function
  - by nature
- how the cost of goods and services is calculated
- the layout of a total cost statement

Set out below are the Performance Criteria covered by this chapter.

PERFORMANCE CRITERIA COVERED

unit 6: RECORDING AND ANALYSING COSTS AND REVENUES

element 6.1

record and analyse information relating to direct costs and revenues

A   identify direct costs in accordance with the organisation's costing procedures

KNOWLEDGE AND UNDERSTANDING – THE BUSINESS ENVIRONMENT

1   the nature and purpose of internal reporting

2   management information requirements

PURPOSE OF COST ACCOUNTING

Cost accounting, as its name implies, enables the managers of a business to know the cost of the firm's output – whether a product or a service – and the revenues from sales. Once costing information is available, managers can use it to assist with

- decision-making
- planning for the future
- control of expenditure

Cost accounting is widely used by all types of businesses – the cost of a hospital operation, the cost of building a new hospital ward, the cost of tuition to a student, the cost of a swim at a sports centre, the cost of a passenger's bus journey, the cost of a new road are all just as important as the cost of making a product. A business – whether it provides a service or makes a product – needs to keep its costs under review; in order to do this it needs accurate cost information. Thus a cost accounting system will provide answers to questions such as:

What does it cost us to provide a student with a day's accountancy course?

What does it cost us to carry out a hip replacement operation?

What does it cost us to make a pair of trainers?

What does it cost us to serve a cheeseburger and fries?

What does it cost us to provide a week's holiday in the Canaries?

The cost accounting system helps managers with production planning and decision-making, such as:

- short-term decisions, eg "how many do we need to make and sell in order to break-even?"; "shall we increase production of Aye or Bee, bearing in mind that shortages of skilled labour mean that we can't do both?"
- long-term decisions, eg "we need to buy a new machine for the factory – shall we buy Machine Exe or Machine Wye?"

The Case Study that follows shows how cost accounting enables the managers of a business to have better information about its activities.

Case Study

S & T MANUFACTURING COMPANY

situation

The following information is given for S & T Manufacturing Company, a two-product (S and T) company, for last year:

			£	£
Sales revenue: S				100,000
T				200,000
				300,000
Less:	Cost of materials	S	50,000	
		T	95,000	
	Labour costs	S	40,000	
		T	50,000	
	*Cost of overheads	S	20,000	
		T	30,000	
				285,000
Profit				15,000

*   Overheads include factory rent, depreciation of machinery, and other production costs.

How would you present this information in a way which will be of more use to the management of the business? What conclusions do you draw for this business?

solution

The information is best presented in a way which analyses the cost and profit of each product:

	S	T	Total
	£	£	£
Cost of materials	50,000	95,000	145,000
Labour costs	40,000	50,000	90,000
Cost of overheads	20,000	30,000	50,000
Total cost	110,000	175,000	285,000
Sales	100,000	200,000	300,000
Less Total cost	110,000	175,000	285,000
Profit/(loss)	(10,000)	25,000	15,000

On the basis of this information, product S should be discontinued because it is making a loss. However, there may be other factors which will have to be considered, eg sales of product T may be linked to sales of S; the overheads of T are likely to increase if S is discontinued because of the way in which the cost of overheads has been split between the two products.

This Case Study emphasises two important functions of cost accounting:

*   to find out the costs (in this case for each product)

*   to give responsibility to someone for those costs (here for the manager of product S to investigate the reasons for the loss of £10,000)

COST ACCOUNTING AND FINANCIAL ACCOUNTING

The Case Study of S & T Manufacturing Company, above, illustrates some of the differences between cost accounting and financial accounting. These two types of accounting, although they produce different reports and statements, obtain their data from the same set of transactions carried out by the business organisation over a given period. This is illustrated in the diagram below.

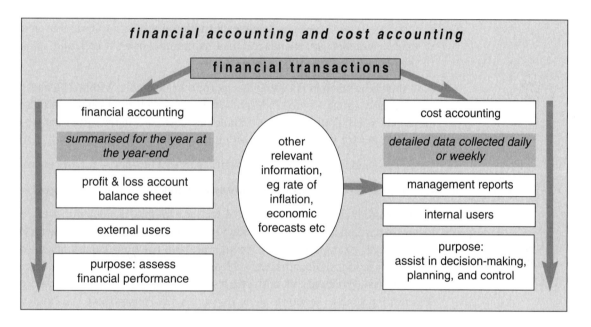

Financial accounting uses the financial data relating to transactions carried out over a period of time. The information is processed through the accounting records and extracted in the form of financial statements – profit and loss account and balance sheet. The statements are often required to be produced by law, eg the Companies Act, and are available to external users such as shareholders, creditors, bank, Inland Revenue, Companies House.

Cost accounting uses the same data to produce reports containing financial information on the recent past and projections for the future. The reports are available to internal users only, such as managers, directors, and owners (but not to shareholders generally). There is no legal requirement to produce this information and the content of the report and the principles used can be suited to the activities of the business or organisation and the requirements of its managers. The information is prepared as frequently as it is required, and speed is often vital as the information may go out-of-date very quickly.

COST UNITS AND COST CENTRES

Before we begin our study of costing we need to understand the terms: cost units and cost centres.

Cost units are units of output to which costs can be charged.

A cost unit can be:

- a unit of production from a factory such as a car, a television, an item of furniture
- a unit of service, such as a passenger-mile on a bus, a transaction on a bank statement, an attendance at a swimming pool, a call unit on a telephone

Care should be taken in choosing the appropriate cost unit. Within a business – particularly in the service industry – there may well be several cost units that can be used. For example, in an hotel the cost units in the restaurant will be meals, and for the rooms, the cost units will be guest nights.

Costs also need to be charged to a specific part of a business – a **cost centre.**

Cost centres are sections of a business to which costs can be charged.

A cost centre in a manufacturing business, for example, is a department of a factory, a particular stage in the production process, or even a whole factory. In a college, examples of cost centres are the teaching departments, or particular sections of departments such as the college's administrative office. In a hospital, examples of cost centres are the hospital wards, operating theatres, specialist sections such as the X-ray department, pathology department.

Collecting costs together in cost centres assists with control of the business or organisation. The manager of a cost centre can be held responsible for its costs.

IDENTIFICATION AND CODING OF COSTS AND REVENUES

coding of costs

Both cost units and cost centres have costs charged to them. This process is carried out in two steps:

- *identification* of the cost unit or cost centre to which the cost is to be charged
- *coding* the cost so that it is charged to the correct cost unit or cost centre

Code numbers are used in cost accounting because:

- they are easier to process than a description of a cost
- once coded there is no doubt as to which cost unit or cost centre the item relates
- they are easily input into a computer accounting system

Various systems are used to code costs. It is for a business to use the system that meets its needs – a smaller business will use a less sophisticated system than does a larger business. Most codes incorporate two sets of numbers that indicate:

- which cost centre or cost unit incurred the cost
- what cost has been used, eg wages, materials

For example, a business uses the following codes:

- code for administration office, 500
- code for sales department, 550
- code for salaries, 200

Thus the cost code for administration salaries is:

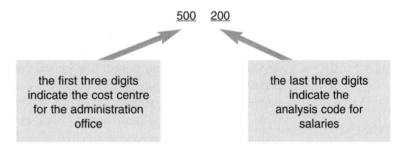

500   200

| the first three digits indicate the cost centre for the administration office | the last three digits indicate the analysis code for salaries |

Using the same principles, the cost code for sales department salaries is 550200. By using coding in this way, the correct cost centre is charged with the cost.

coding of revenues

In a similar way to coding of costs, revenue from sales needs to be coded so that information is available to management on:

- which product has been sold
- which department, or salesperson, made the sale

For example, a restaurant uses the following codes:

- code for revenue from meals, 700
- code for revenue from the bar, 800
- code for Jason, a waiter, 082

Thus the revenue code for meals sold by Jason is:

<u>082</u> <u>700</u>

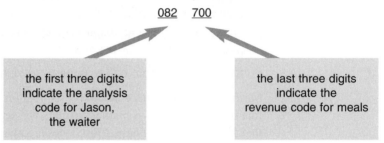

| the first three digits indicate the analysis code for Jason, the waiter | the last three digits indicate the revenue code for meals |

Using the same principles, the revenue code for bar sales made by Jason is 082800.

You can often see the use of revenue codes in use in a shop, or a bar, or a restaurant – the salesperson first keys in his or her personal code number on the till and then records the items sold by either scanning them through a bar code reader, or by pressing the appropriate keys. The information on sales revenues is then available to the managers of the business.

features of a good coding system

The source documents for coding vary depending on the type of cost or revenue – examples of common sources of data are given on page 29. Within the costing department of a business or organisation, it is necessary to code documents received and issued. The person carrying out the coding – the coding clerk – will use the organisation's *coding manual,* or the *policy manual* (the book that states how all operations within the organisation are to be carried out). They must work to high standards of accuracy – wrong coding will lead to incorrect information being supplied to managers, which could in turn lead to wrong decision-making.

The way in which documents are coded varies from one organisation to another. For some, the code number is written on the document and marked clearly; others use a rubber stamp to provide a layout on which can be indicated the code number and the initials of the person entering the code.

For a coding system to work well:

- coding should follow a logical sequence – similar items, such as cost centres, should be grouped together within the coding system
- codes should be unique, ie a particular code number should relate only to one item going to one particular cost/revenue centre
- codes should provide the correct level of detail, ie the cost/revenue centre code and the analysis code
- coding of documents must be accurate
- code numbers must be complete, ie the full code to be indicated and not just the cost/revenue centre code or the analysis code

- coding of documents must be carried out regularly within the timescales required by the organisation

The objective of coding is to provide correct analysis so as to give information from the costing system to managers. By analysing costs and income to cost/revenue centres we can answer questions such as "how much was basic pay in the sales department last month?"; "how much was factory overtime last week?"; "what sales did the Birmingham office make of product Exe last month?"

CLASSIFICATION OF COSTS

Within any business, whether it manufactures a product or provides a service, there are certain costs involved at various stages to produce the units of output. The diagram below shows the costs of a manufacturing business which are incurred by the three main sections or 'areas' of a manufacturing business.

These three separate sections are:

- **factory** – where production takes place and the product is 'finished' and made ready for selling
- **warehouse** – where finished goods are stored and from where they are despatched when they are sold
- **office** – where the support functions take place – marketing, sales, administration, finance and so on

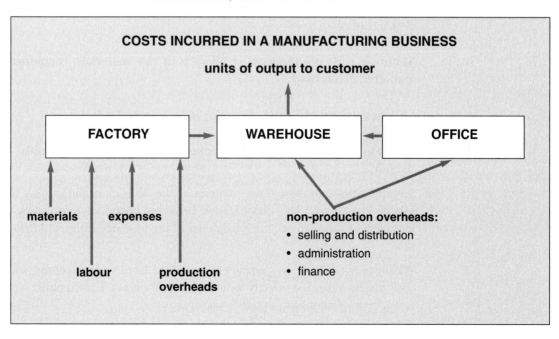

Note that while the diagram on the previous page shows the costs of a manufacturing business, it can be adapted easily to fit non-manufacturing organisations, such as a shop, a hospital, a school or college, a church, a club. While the units of output of these organisations differ from those of a manufacturer, nevertheless they still incur costs at various stages of the 'production' process.

In order to prepare information for the managers of a business, costs must be *classified*, ie organised into sets in a way which the managers will find useful.

This can be done in three ways:

- by element
- by function
- by nature

classification of costs by element

Businesses and organisations incur many different kinds of cost in the production of goods or 'output', including costs of the warehouse and the office. The most basic way of splitting up costs is according to the type of expenditure under the headings:

- materials, eg the components to make a car
- labour, eg wages of an employee
- expenses, eg rent and rates, telephone charges, insurance

Note: material, labour, and expenses are often referred to as the three elements of cost.

Materials costs are the costs of all sorts of raw materials, components and other goods used.

Labour costs are the costs of employees' wages and salaries.

Expenses are other costs, which cannot be included in 'materials' or 'labour'.

Splitting costs into these three elements applies to both manufacturing and service businesses. The classification provides important information to managers as they can see the breakdown of the total into different kinds of cost.

Within each of the three elements of materials, labour and expenses, some costs can be identified directly with each unit of output. For example:

- the cost of components used in making cars

- the wages of workers on a production line in a factory

These are termed **direct costs**. In manufacturing, the total of all the direct costs is called the **prime cost** of the output.

A direct cost is a cost that can be identified directly with each unit of output.

Prime cost is the total of all direct costs.

Costs which cannot be identified directly with each unit of output are **indirect costs** or overheads.

Indirect costs (overheads) are all costs other than those identified as 'direct costs'. They cannot be identified directly with specific units of output.

There are many examples of overheads, including:
- telephone charges
- insurance premiums
- cost of wages of non-production staff, such as managers, secretaries, cost accountants and so on
- running costs of delivery vehicles
- depreciation charge for fixed assets

Note particularly the last two examples. In cost accounting, as in financial accounting, we distinguish between capital and revenue expenditure. In our analysis of costs we are referring to revenue expenditure, and therefore include the running costs and depreciation of fixed assets, rather than the capital cost of their purchase.

We now have six possible classifications for costs, each of the three elements of materials, labour and expenses being split into direct and indirect costs. These are illustrated for a manufacturing business in the table on the next page, while the Case Study on page 22 is for a service business.

classification of costs by function

Another method of classifying costs is to look at the costs incurred in different sections of the organisation, according to their 'function', or the kind of work being done.

In manufacturing, the main function is *production* of the goods. The business could not be run, however, without secretaries, administrators, accountants, sales and delivery staff and so on – these are examples of *non-production* costs.

	DIRECT COSTS	INDIRECT COSTS
MATERIALS	The cost of raw materials from which the finished product is made.	The cost of all other materials, eg grease for machines, cleaning materials.
LABOUR	Wages paid to those who work the machinery on the production line or who are involved in assembly or finishing of the product.	Wages and salaries paid to all other employees, eg managers and supervisors, maintenance staff, administration staff.
EXPENSES	Any expenses which can be attributed to particular units of output, eg royalties payable to the designer of a product, fees linked directly to specific output and paid to people who are not employees.	All other expenses, eg rent, rates, telephone, lighting and heating costs, depreciation of fixed assets, insurance, advertising, etc. These are costs which cannot be linked directly with units of output.
TOTAL	**TOTAL DIRECT COST = PRIME COST**	**TOTAL INDIRECT COST = TOTAL OVERHEADS**

When costs are classified by function, the main headings generally used are:

production

administration

selling and distribution ⎤

finance ⎦ ─── non-production costs

Other functions can be added to suit the needs of a particular business. For example, a 'Research and Development' heading could be used if a company spent large sums of money in researching and developing new products.

Non-manufacturing organisations – such as a hospital or a college – may use other 'function' headings, according to the kind of work each section of the organisation carries out.

Please note that, in classifying costs by their function, we are looking at the same set of costs for the organisation as before. We are simply presenting them in different groupings.

It is an important function of accounting that information should be presented in the form most suitable for the purpose for which it is required. For some management purposes, classification of costs by function provides better information.

classification of costs by nature

In cost accounting, it is important to appreciate the nature of costs – in particular to understand that not all costs increase or decrease directly in line with increases or decreases in output. By nature, costs are:

- fixed, or
- semi-variable, or
- variable

The diagram below shows the differences between these.

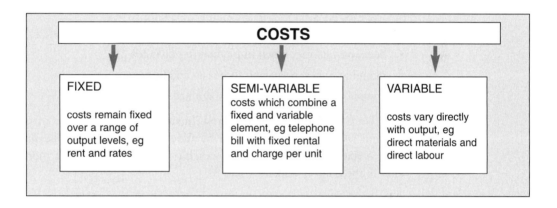

It is important to know the nature of costs and how they are affected by changes in the level of output. For example, a business decides to increase its output by 25% – will all costs increase by 25%? Fixed costs, such as rent and rates, are likely to remain unchanged, provided that there is capacity for the increased output within the existing building. Variable costs, such as direct materials and direct labour, are likely to increase by 25% as they generally vary directly with output (unless any economies of scale can be achieved). Semi-variable costs, such as the telephone bill, will increase as the extra business generates more 'phone calls; however, the increase should certainly be much less than 25%.

REASONS FOR CLASSIFYING COSTS

The question might be asked, "Why classify costs in three ways?" The answer is that we can see the same business from three different viewpoints – this will help management to run the business better:

- **by element**

  looking for the high cost elements in order to make savings, eg labour might be identified as being too high

- **by function**

  looking at the different departments to see which are the high-spending departments – perhaps savings can be made

- **by nature**

  identifying the costs as being fixed, semi-variable, or variable – the business might be able to make savings by altering the balance between fixed and variable costs

Thus classifying costs helps management with:

- decision-making, when implementing changes
- planning, when preparing forecasts and budgets
- control, when checking results against what was planned

The two Case Studies which follow illustrate the classification of costs by element (Albion Restaurant) and by function (Thyme plc). The nature of costs – fixed, semi-variable, and variable will be considered in more detail later in the book (Chapters 4 and 8).

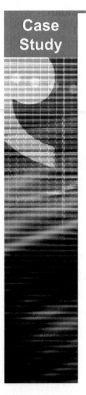

Case Study

ALBION RESTAURANT:
COST CLASSIFICATION BY ELEMENT

situation

Albion Restaurant is a large restaurant. Some of the costs incurred by Albion Restaurant are listed below:

(a) wages of the cleaner

(b) cost of heating the restaurant

(c) wages of the chefs

(d) telephone charges

(e) paper table covers and napkins

(f) cost of ingredients for meals

(g) cleaning materials

(h) advertising costs

(i) maintenance contract for ovens

(j) wages of waiters and waitresses

As an accounts assistant at Albion Restaurant, you are to:

• suggest a suitable cost unit for a restaurant.

• classify the costs into the six categories shown in the table below; give your answer by entering the costs into the table:

	DIRECT COSTS	INDIRECT COSTS
MATERIALS		
LABOUR		
EXPENSES		

solution

An appropriate cost unit for a restaurant would be one meal.

	DIRECT COSTS	INDIRECT COSTS
MATERIALS	(f) cost of ingredients for meals	(e) paper table covers and napkins (g) cleaning materials
LABOUR	(c) wages of the chefs (j) wages of waiters and waitresses*	(a) wages of the cleaner
EXPENSES		(b) cost of heating the restaurant (d) telephone charges (h) advertising costs (i) maintenance contract for ovens

* see next page

* You may have classified (j) 'wages of waiters and waitresses' as 'indirect wages'. This is an equally valid answer. A cost accounting system is designed to suit a particular organisation. There are some costs that may be treated as either direct or indirect costs, depending on the particular situation and the information required from the system. Costs which could be linked directly to cost units may be treated as overheads if this is easier and saves time without losing any useful information. Whichever treatment is used, it is important to be consistent so that, next time the cost is incurred, it is dealt with in the same way.

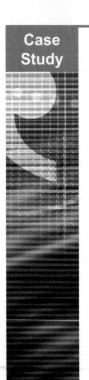

Case Study

THYME PLC:
COST CLASSIFICATION BY FUNCTION

situation

Thyme plc is a manufacturer of TV sets.

Some of the indirect costs incurred by Thyme plc are listed below:

(a)   depreciation charge for delivery vehicles

(b)   salary of the personnel manager

(c)   materials used for maintaining factory machinery

(d)   cost of computer disks for office computers

(e)   interest payable on a bank overdraft

(f)   salary of the sales manager

(g)   cost of power used for running factory machinery

(h)   maintenance contract for office photocopier

As an accounts assistant at Thyme, you are to classify the costs by function and give your answer by entering the costs into a table.

solution

PRODUCTION COSTS	(c) materials used for maintaining factory machinery (g) cost of power used for running factory machinery
SELLING AND DISTRIBUTION COSTS	(a) depreciation charge for delivery vehicles (f) salary of the sales manager
ADMINISTRATION COSTS	(b) salary of the personnel manager (d) cost of computer disks for office computers (h) maintenance contract for office photocopier
FINANCE COSTS	(e) interest payable on a bank overdraft

CALCULATING THE COST OF GOODS AND SERVICES

Using the principles of costing will help to calculate the cost of a product – whether goods or services. Only when the cost of producing each unit of output is known, can a business make decisions about the selling price.

The steps towards calculating the cost of goods and services are:

identify the unit of output

The cost units for a particular business or organisation must be identified. As we have seen earlier, these are the units of output to which costs can be charged. Only by recovering costs through the sales of output can a business make a profit.

calculate the number of units of output for a particular time period

Once the unit of output is identified, the business is then able to calculate how many units can be produced or provided in a given time period, such as a day, week, month, quarter or year. For example, a garage will work out how many hours of mechanics' time are available, or a car manufacturer will calculate how many cars it can produce in a year.

calculate the direct costs for a particular time period

Having established the number of units of output for a particular time period, the next task is to calculate the direct costs, or prime cost, for that time period. As we have seen earlier in this chapter, the direct costs comprise:

direct materials	identifiable with the product
direct labour	the wages paid to those who make the product
direct expenses	attributable to the product

The amounts of the direct costs are added together to give the total direct costs (prime cost) of the output for the time period.

calculate the indirect costs for a particular time period

The indirect costs, or overheads, of the production or service must be calculated for the particular time period. Indirect costs comprise:

> *indirect materials*   materials used that are not attributed directly to production
>
> *indirect labour*   wages and salaries paid to those who are not directly involved in production
>
> *indirect expenses*   expenses of the business not attributed directly to production

Once the indirect costs have been calculated, we must then ensure that their total cost is charged to the cost units for a particular time period. Only by including indirect costs in the total cost of the output can a business recover their cost from the sales made.

The amounts of the indirect costs are added together to give the total indirect costs (overheads) for the time period.

calculate the total cost of a unit of output

Once the direct and indirect costs for a time period are known, the total cost of a unit of output can be calculated, as follows:

$$\frac{direct\ costs + indirect\ costs}{number\ of\ units\ of\ output} = total\ cost\ of\ a\ unit\ of\ output$$

The total cost is also known as the absorption cost – because it absorbs (includes) both the direct costs and the indirect costs. Once total cost is known, the business can use the information to help it make pricing and other decisions. Note that, for stock valuation purposes, only those indirect costs which relate to production are to be included in total cost (see page 58).

calculating the cost – a summary

The process of calculating the cost of output is illustrated in the diagram shown on the next page.

costs for a service business

While the units of 'output' of businesses or organisations that produce a service are not manufactured products, they still incur the costs of:

*   materials
*   labour
*   expenses

Some of the costs of a service business can be linked directly to the 'output' or the cost units of the organisation, but others are classified as overheads.

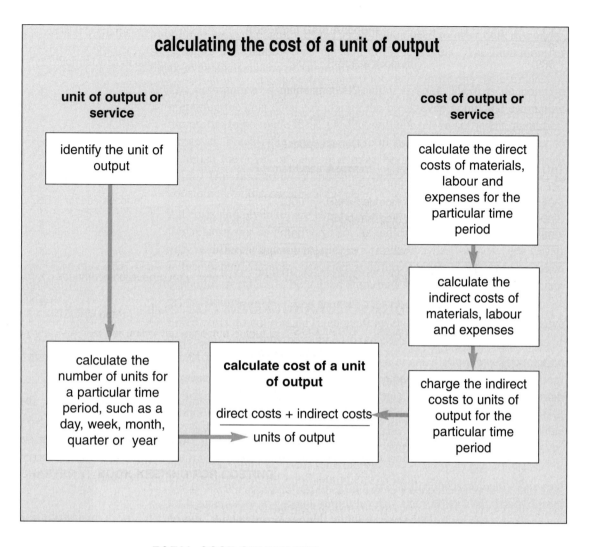

calculating the cost of a unit of output

unit of output or service

identify the unit of output

calculate the number of units for a particular time period, such as a day, week, month, quarter or year

calculate cost of a unit of output

$$\frac{\text{direct costs} + \text{indirect costs}}{\text{units of output}}$$

cost of output or service

calculate the direct costs of materials, labour and expenses for the particular time period

calculate the indirect costs of materials, labour and expenses

charge the indirect costs to units of output for the particular time period

TOTAL COST STATEMENT

The total cost statement brings together all the costs involved in producing the output of a business. It can be prepared on the basis of:

- a single cost unit, eg the cost of making one car in a car factory

- a batch, eg the cost of making 1,000 'special edition' cars

- the whole factory, eg the cost of all the car factory's output for a given time period

The total cost statement is prepared using the following layout:

```
┌─────────────────────────────────────────────────────────────────────┐
│              TOTAL COST STATEMENT                                     │
│                                                               £       │
│                                                                       │
│           Direct materials                                    x       │
│                                                                       │
│   add     Direct labour                                       x       │
│                                                                       │
│   add     Direct expenses                                    _x_      │
│                                                                       │
│   equals  PRIME COST                                          x       │
│                                                                       │
│   add     Production overheads                               _x_      │
│                                                                       │
│   equals  PRODUCTION COST                                     x       │
│                                                                       │
│   add     Selling and distribution costs ⌐                   x       │
│                                                                       │
│   add     Administration costs ─────────┼── non-production   x       │
│                                              overheads                │
│   add     Finance costs ─────────────────┘                   x       │
│                                                              ___      │
│   equals  TOTAL COST                                          x       │
│                                                              ═══      │
└─────────────────────────────────────────────────────────────────────┘
```

Note that:

- *prime cost* is the direct cost of manufacturing products, before the addition of production overheads
- *production cost* is the factory cost of manufacturing the products, ie prime cost plus production (factory) overheads
- *total cost* is production cost plus non-production overheads

The cost structure above is especially appropriate for a manufacturing business; indeed a separate *manufacturing account* – which shows costs through to production cost – is prepared prior to the profit and loss account. Manufacturing accounts are covered in more detail in Chapter 7.

By taking total cost away from sales revenue we can create a profit statement. This shows the profitability of the business after all costs have been taken into account. The profit statement is:

```
┌─────────────────────────────────────────────────────────────────────┐
│              PROFIT STATEMENT                                         │
│                                                               £       │
│                                                                       │
│           Sales revenue                                       x       │
│                                                                       │
│   less    Total cost                                          x       │
│                                                              ___      │
│   equals  PROFIT                                              x       │
│                                                              ═══      │
└─────────────────────────────────────────────────────────────────────┘
```

SOURCES OF DATA FOR COSTING

In order to code, analyse and classify costs and revenues we need to obtain the information from a data source. There will be many of these within a business or organisation – potential sources include:

- materials
  - purchase orders
  - goods received notes
  - returns notes
  - invoices received
  - materials requisitions
  - stock records
  - job sheets
  - ledgers

- labour
  - clock and time cards
  - payroll analysis sheets
  - income tax and National Insurance Contributions
  - job sheets
  - ledgers

- expenses
  - invoices received
  - receipts
  - cash book
  - petty cash book
  - cheque counterfoils
  - bank transfers made
  - bank statements
  - ledgers

- income
  - invoices issued
  - cash receipts issued
  - bank paying-in book
  - bank transfers received
  - bank statements
  - ledgers

Note: at this stage in your studies you may not be familiar with all these sources of data – specialist terms will be explained in subsequent chapters.

Chapter Summary

- Cost accounting is essential to provide information for managers of organisations in order to assist with decision-making, planning and control.

- Costs may be charged directly to cost units or to sections of the business defined as cost centres.

- Costs may be classified by element, or by function, or by nature, depending on the purpose for which the information is required.

- The three categories of cost: materials, labour and expenses can each be split into direct costs and indirect costs. Indirect costs are also called 'overheads'. This gives a six-way split of costs:

DIRECT MATERIALS	INDIRECT MATERIALS
DIRECT LABOUR	INDIRECT LABOUR
DIRECT EXPENSES	INDIRECT EXPENSES
TOTAL DIRECT COSTS or PRIME COST	TOTAL OVERHEADS

- Overheads may be classified by dividing them amongst the functions or sections of the business:
  - factory (or production)
  - selling and distribution
  - administration
  - finance
  - other section headings as appropriate to the organisation

- By nature, costs are fixed, or semi-variable, or variable.

- Total cost of producing a unit of output $= \dfrac{\text{direct costs} + \text{indirect costs}}{\text{number of units of output}}$

- A total cost statement lists the total of the direct costs and the overheads. Sales revenue minus total cost equals profit.

Key Terms

cost unit	unit of output to which costs can be charged
cost centre	section of a business to which costs can be charged
materials costs	the costs of all sorts of raw materials, components and other goods used
labour costs	the costs of employees' wages and salaries
expenses	other costs, which cannot be included in 'materials' or 'labour'
direct cost	a cost that can be identified directly with each unit of output

indirect cost (overhead)	a cost that cannot be identified directly with each unit of output
prime cost	the total of all direct costs
fixed costs	costs which remain fixed over a range of output levels
semi-variable costs	costs which combine a fixed and variable element
variable costs	costs which vary directly with output
total cost statement	list of the total of the direct costs and the overhead

Student Activities

1.1 Select an organisation – either where you work, or one with which you are familiar.

(a) Prepare a diagram, similar to that shown on page 17, identifying the main functions of the organisation and the costs incurred by each section.

(b) Describe the cost units and cost centres used by the organisation.

1.2 Suggest one cost unit and two cost centres for:

- a college of further education

- a mixed farm, growing crops and raising cattle

1.3 (a) Why is it important to analyse costs in different ways, eg by element, by function and by nature?

(b) Classify each of the following costs by nature (ie fixed, or semi-variable, or variable):

- raw materials

- factory rent

- telephone

- direct labour, eg production workers paid on the basis of work done

- indirect labour, eg supervisors' salaries

- commission paid to sales staff

Taking the costs in turn, explain to a friend, who is about to set up a furniture manufacturing business, why you have classified each as fixed, or semi-variable, or variable. Answer the comment, "What difference does it make anyway, they are all costs that have to be paid."

1.4 Severn Manufacturing Limited makes chairs for school and college use. The chairs have plastic seats, and tubular steel legs. You are to classify the manufacturing costs into:

- direct materials
- indirect materials
- direct labour
- indirect labour
- direct expenses
- indirect expenses

The cost items to be classified are:

COST ITEM	CLASSIFICATION (write your answer)
Tubular steel	
Factory supervisor's salary	
Wages of employee operating the moulding machine which produces the chair seats	
Works canteen assistant's wages	
Rates of factory	
Power to operate machines	
Factory heating and lighting	
Plastic for making chair seats	
Hire of special machinery for one particular order	
Cost of grease for the moulding machine	
Depreciation of factory machinery	
Depreciation of office equipment	

If you believe alternative classifications exist, argue the case and state if you need further information from the company.

1.5   Betterwell NHS Trust is a large hospital with many departments. Costs of the general operating theatre have been identified and you are to classify them into:

- direct materials

- indirect materials

- direct labour

- indirect labour

- direct expenses

- indirect expenses

The cost items to be classified are:

COST ITEM	CLASSIFICATION (write your answer)
Dressings	
Disposable scalpels	
Surgeon's salary	
Floor cleaning materials	
Laundry	
Depreciation of staff drinks machine	
Theatre heat and light	
Porter's wages	
Anaesthetic gas	
Depreciation of theatre equipment	
Maintenance of theatre equipment	
Cost of CDs for music in theatre	
Anaesthetist's salary	

If you believe alternative classifications exist, argue the case and state if you need further information.

1.6 Wyvern Water Limited bottles natural spring water at its plant at Walcoll at the base of the Wyvern Hills. The natural spring is on land owned by a local farmer to whom a royalty is paid for each bottle of water produced.

You are working in the costing section of Wyvern Water and are asked to analyse the following cost items into the appropriate columns and to agree the totals:

Cost item	Total cost	Prime cost	Production overheads	Admin costs	Selling and distribution costs
	£	£	£	£	£
Wages of employees working on the bottling line	6,025				
Wages of employees in the stores department	2,750				
Cost of bottles	4,050				
Safety goggles for bottling line employees	240				
Advertisement for new employees	125				
Depreciation of bottling machinery	500				
Depreciation of sales staff's cars	1,000				
Royalty paid to local farmer	750				
Cost of trade exhibition	1,500				
Computer stationery	210				
Sales staff salaries	4,095				
TOTALS	21,245				

1.7 The following figures relate to the accounts of Hughes Limited, a manufacturing business, for the year ended 31 December 2007:

	£
Raw materials used in the factory	118,830
Rent and rates of factory	16,460
Factory wages	117,315
Factory power	3,825
Factory heat and light	1,185
Factory expenses and maintenance	4,095
Salaries and wages of office staff	69,350
Advertising	11,085
Office expenses	3,930
Depreciation of factory plant and machinery	3,725
Sales revenue	426,350

You are to:

(a) Prepare a total cost statement for the year which shows:

- prime cost
- production cost
- total cost

Discuss any assumptions that you make and state if you need further information from the company.

(b) Prepare a profit statement for the year (on the assumption that all the goods manufactured have been sold).

2 Materials costs

this chapter covers . . .

Businesses and other organisations hold stocks of materials in the form of raw materials and components, products bought for resale, and service items. Often the value of such materials is high, representing a considerable investment of money. In this chapter we look at:

- the purchasing and control of stocks of materials
- re-ordering procedures
- the records that are kept for stocks of materials
- the purposes of stock taking and stock reconciliation
- the valuation of stock
- the use of stores ledger records
- the book-keeping entries for materials costs

PERFORMANCE CRITERIA COVERED

unit 6: RECORDING AND ANALYSING COSTS AND REVENUES

element 6.1

record and analyse information relating to direct costs and revenues

A   identify direct costs in accordance with the organisation's costing procedures

B   record and analyse information relating to direct costs

C   calculate direct costs in accordance with the organisation's policies and procedures

D   check cost information for stocks against usage and stock control practices

E   resolve or refer queries to the appropriate person

MATERIALS STOCKS

Materials is the cost of:

- raw materials and components bought for use by a manufacturing business
- products bought for resale by a shop or a wholesaler
- service items, such as stationery, bought for use within a business or organisation

In costing we need to distinguish between direct materials and indirect materials. Thus a manufacturer classifies the cost of materials from which the finished product is made as direct materials; other materials used – grease for machines, cleaning materials, etc – are classified as indirect materials, and form part of the overheads of the business.

The buying of materials is normally undertaken by a firm's Purchasing Department, although in smaller businesses the responsibility will be carried out by an individual or the owner. The job of the buyer(s) is to ensure that the purchases made by the business are bought at the lowest possible cost, consistent with quality and quantity.

At any time, most businesses will hold materials in stock ready for use or resale. The diagram shown on the next page examines the holding of stocks by three types of business: a manufacturing business which makes stock, a trading business such as a shop, which buys and sells stock, and a service business or organisation.

PLANNING OF PURCHASES AND CONTROL OF STOCKS

Planning for the purchase of materials and the control of stocks of materials is critical to the efficiency of a business. However, holding stocks is expensive:

- they have to be financed, possibly by using borrowed money (on which interest is payable)
- there are storage costs, including rent and rates, security, insurance

Within an organisation there are conflicting demands on its policy for stocks of materials. On the one hand, the finance department will want to minimise stock levels to keep costs as low as possible; on the other hand, production and marketing departments will be anxious to keep stocks high so that output can be maintained and new orders satisfied speedily before customers decide to buy elsewhere.

STOCKS HELD BY BUSINESSES

Manufacturing Business	Trading Business	Service Business
raw materials and components	**goods for sale**	**consumable materials**
These stocks are held by a manufacturer to reduce the risk of production delays if a supplier fails to deliver on time. A vehicle manufacturer may hold a stock of plastic bumpers, for example.	These are items the retailer or wholesaler has bought in (eg from the manufacturer) and has available for sale to the customer. For example:	These are materials that are either for use in the organisation or for sale to the customer as part of the service provided. For example:
work-in-progress These are stocks of part-finished goods on the production line. In a car factory these would be cars partly assembled, for example.	■ *retailers* a supermarket will have a stock of cans of orange drink for sale ■ *wholesalers* a timber merchant will have quantities of wood for sale to customers	■ *for use in the organisation* in a college there will be a stock of paper for the photocopiers ■ *items for sale* an optician will sell reading glasses as part of the service provided
finished goods These are goods that have been completed and are ready for sale to customers. A vehicle manufacturer would have completed cars ready for sale, for example.		

There are a number of methods of planning purchases and of stock control. Which is adopted will depend on the size and sophistication of the organisation. It is important that an organisation knows how much stock it has at any time – either by making a physical stock count, or by keeping computer records (which need physical verification at regular intervals) – and it must know when it will have to re-order more stocks. The organisation then needs to know the quantity that needs to be re-ordered. The methods used include:

estimation   Some small businesses do not keep much stock, and the owner may estimate the quantity and timing of materials purchases. This is not a recommended method for a well-managed business or organisation.

'two bin' system   The principle here is to keep two 'bins' of a stock unit. When the first bin has run out, new stocks of materials are ordered and will be supplied before the second 'bin' runs out. The term 'bin' is used loosely, and can apply to any measure of stock. This is a very basic principle, but it works well in many situations.

perpetual inventory   'Inventory' is another word for stock. This system records receipt and issue of stock as the items pass in and out of the organisation, and re-orders are made accordingly. Records of stock are kept manually, or more commonly now on computer file activated by reading of bar codes. Many supermarkets and manufacturing businesses work on this basis, and order stock on a 'Just-In-Time' basis (see page 43).

formulas   Organisations need to calculate when to order materials, and how much to order; formulas can be used to help with this. These are explained in the sections which follow.

MATERIALS PURCHASES: LEVEL METHOD OF RE-ORDERING

This method orders materials in fixed quantities, eg 750 reams of photocopying paper (a ream is 500 sheets). For such a system to operate, the organisation should know:

- the *lead time*, ie how long it takes for new stock to be delivered after being ordered
- the appropriate *re-order quantity*
- the *minimum stock level,* ie the lowest level that stock should fall to before the new order from the supplier is delivered (the minimum stock level is also known as a *buffer stock* to meet unexpected emergencies)
- the *maximum stock level* that can be held – this can be calculated (see below) but may well be determined by the amount of storage space available in the warehouse, shop or office stationery 'cupboard'
- the *re-order level*, ie the point at which a new order is to be placed – this is often the most critical factor to determine

Many organisations use manual or computer stock control systems to keep a running record of the amount of each material held in stock, the lead time for re-ordering, and the minimum stock level. The level method of re-ordering is illustrated as follows:

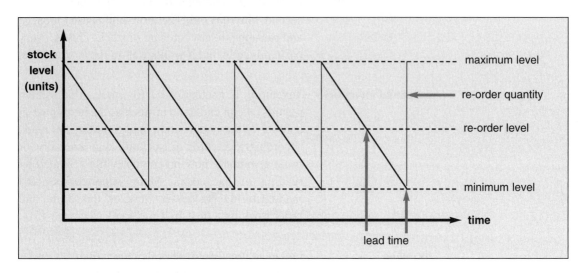

re-order level

The re-order level is calculated so that replacement materials will be delivered just as the stock level reaches the minimum level. The calculation of re-order level is:

(maximum usage ✗ maximum lead time) + minimum stock level

re-order quantity

At the re-order level, a purchase order for new stock is forwarded to the supplier. The quantity to be purchased is the re-order quantity; which is calculated as:

maximum stock level − minimum stock level

maximum and minimum stock levels

By the time new stock is delivered, the remaining stock should have fallen to the minimum level, so that the new stock restores the level to the maximum.

The maximum and minimum stock levels can be set as follows:

• *maximum stock level = minimum stock level + re-order quantity*

• *minimum stock level = re-order level − (average usage ✗ average lead time)*

However, maximum stock may be determined by other factors, eg the amount of storage space available, a policy decision not to hold more than a certain number of days' (or weeks' or months') usage.

example

A4, white photocopying paper

daily usage	30 reams (a ream is 500 sheets)
lead time	5 days
re-order quantity	750 reams*
minimum stock level	150 reams**
maximum stock level	900 reams***

Re-order level = (30 daily usage x 5 days' lead time) + 150 minimum stock

= (30 x 5) + 150

= 150 + 150

= 300 reams (re-order level)

When the balance of stock falls to 300 reams, a purchase order for 750 reams is forwarded to the supplier of the paper.

* re-order quantity = maximum stock level – minimum stock level

= 900 – 150

= 750 reams

** minimum stock level = re-order level – (average usage x average lead time)

= 300 – (30 x 5 days)

= 150 reams

*** maximum stock level = minimum stock level + re-order quantity

= 150 + 750 = 900 reams

It is important not to treat stock calculations in isolation – there does need to be consideration of wider issues which may affect the business or organisation. Such issues include:

- needs of the business – for example, if a stock item is being used less frequently than before, the stock calculations will need to be revised to suit current and future needs

- obsolescence of stock – for example, if spare parts are kept for a particular make and model of vehicle, stock levels will need to be run down if the vehicles are being replaced by those of a different make and model

- seasonal variations affecting usage and stock levels – for example, a business using oil for heating may be offered a cheaper price when usage is low in the summer which may make it worthwhile to stock up; by contrast, when usage is high in the winter, the supplier's price and lead times may increase

MATERIALS PURCHASES: ECONOMIC ORDER QUANTITY (EOQ)

It is clear that the re-order quantity is critical to the efficiency of stock-holding:

- if re-order amounts are *too large*, too much stock will be held, which will be an expense to the business
- if re-order amounts are *too small*, the expense of constantly re-ordering will outweigh any cost savings of lower stock levels, and there will be the danger that the item might 'run out'

The most economic re-order quantity – *the economic order quantity (EOQ)* – can be calculated by a mathematical formula which involves a number of different costs and other figures:

- *ordering cost* – the administration cost of placing each order, eg stationery, postage, wages, telephone
- *stock holding cost* – the cost of keeping the stock on the shelves expressed as the cost of holding one item of stock per year; examples of stock holding costs include rent and rates, insurance, wages, deterioration, obsolescence, security
- *annual usage* – the number of stock units used per year

The formula is:

$$\text{Economic Order Quantity (EOQ)} = \sqrt{\frac{2 \times \text{annual usage} \times \text{ordering cost}}{\text{stock holding cost}}}$$

On a calculator with a square root function, this formula can be worked out easily. Calculate the figures in the formula first, and then press the square root button ($\sqrt{}$).

For example, for a particular stock item, the ordering cost of each order is £30, the stock holding cost is £2 per stock item per year, and annual usage is 2,000 units. The EOQ formula is applied as follows:

$$\text{Economic Order Quantity (EOQ)} = \sqrt{\frac{2 \times 2{,}000 \times £30}{£2}}$$

$$= \sqrt{\frac{120{,}000}{2}}$$

continued on next page

$$= \sqrt{60,000}$$

$$= \quad 245 \text{ units}$$

As a result of using EOQ, a balance is struck between the cost of placing an order and the cost of holding stock; EOQ represents the most efficient level of order to place – in the example here it is 245 units.

As well as the formula method, EOQ can be found using other methods – by tabulation and by graph.

MATERIALS PURCHASES: JUST-IN-TIME (JIT)

Just-In-Time is a system of materials purchasing favoured by manufacturing businesses and large supermarket chains. Using JIT, materials needed by a manufacturer are delivered to the production line, or – for retailers – delivered to the store, just as they are needed. The essentials of the successful operation of JIT are:

• the right quantities

• in the right place

• just-in-time

For JIT to operate effectively, the manufacturer or supermarket needs quality suppliers who can be contracted to deliver materials in accordance with demand schedules. In this way stock levels are kept to a minimum, with consequent savings in stock holding costs. The disadvantage is that the JIT system is susceptible to supply chain problems – eg bad weather or a labour dispute – there are no buffer stocks to absorb such difficulties.

Manufacturers who use JIT often try to attract component suppliers to the same area. The car manufacturer Fiat has gone a step further than this by building a car factory in southern Italy with the component firms on the same site.

Retailers who use JIT – such as major supermarket chains – have arrangements with their suppliers to supply goods more or less on demand. Information technology systems used by these businesses help them to anticipate the quantities they have to order: electronic tills provide up-to-the-minute stock usage for each product 'line' and so stock levels are constantly monitored. Orders are sent to suppliers, often through EDI (Electronic Data Interchange) systems, and delivered within a short space of time. If there is a run on a particular item – eg soft drinks in a heat wave – the system will ensure that new stock is delivered very rapidly.

Factors to consider in relation to JIT include:

- reliability of the supplier
- quality of goods supplied
- effect on the business of disruption of supplies caused by factors such as bad weather or strikes
- flexibility of suppliers to react positively to changes in orders caused by increases or decreases in demand
- minimal stock taking requirements
- alternative uses for resources released, eg storage areas no longer needed
- overall efficiency of the JIT system in the context of maintaining the firm's output

STOCK RECORDS

Most organisations will have records of their stocks of materials. Such records may be kept either by using a computer stock control system, or manually on individual stock records. Under both methods – computer and manual – a separate record is maintained for each of the different materials kept in stock. The system is used whether the materials are held for resale by a retailer, or for use in production by a manufacturer. When supplies of the material are received they are entered in the stock record, and when items are sold (or issued to production) they are deducted from the stock record.

A typical stock record is shown on the next page. The stock item is A4 white photocopying paper which is used within the organisation.

Note the following on the stock record:

stock description	refers to the description of the stock, for example photocopying paper
stock units	refers to how the stock is stored or packed, eg photocopying paper is packed in reams (packets of 500 sheets)
stock reference no	refers to the identification number allocated to the stock by the business – often marked on the stock, and sometimes by means of a barcode
location	refers to where the stock can be found in the stores, eg row A, bin 6 refers to the location in the storeroom or warehouse

STOCK RECORD

Stock description .. A4 white photocopying paper ....

Stock units .... reams ....

Stock ref. No. .... P1026 ....

Location .... row A, bin 6 ....

Minimum .... 150 reams	
Maximum .... 900 reams	
Re-order level .... 300 reams	
Re-order quantity .... 750 reams	

DATE	GOODS RECEIVED		GOODS ISSUED		BALANCE
	Reference	Quantity	Reference	Quantity	
2007					
1 Apr					300
2 Apr			MR 101	40	260
5 Apr			MR 104	30	230
6 Apr			MR 116	50	180
7 Apr			MR 121	40	140
8 Apr	GRN 17901	750			890
9 Apr	MRN 58	5			895

goods received the two columns record the Goods Received Note (GRN) reference and the quantity of items received – or where goods are returned into stock, the reference of the Materials Returns Note (MRN)

goods issued the two columns record the Materials Requisition (MR) reference and the number of items issued; an example of a Materials Requisition is shown below

balance is the number of items which remain in stock

MATERIALS REQUISITION

Department: Printing

Document no: MR 101

Date: 2 April 2007

Code no	Description	Quantity	For cost office use only Value of issue (£)
P 1026	A4 white photocopying paper	40 reams	

Authorised by: *R Omar*   Received by: *Pete Bashir*

STOCK TAKING AND STOCK RECONCILIATION

stock taking

A business or organisation will check regularly that the quantity of stock held is the same as the number recorded on the stock records. This is done by means of a stock take – counting the physical stock on hand to check against the balance shown by the records, and to identify any theft or deterioration.

Stock taking is carried out on either a periodic basis or continuously.

A *periodic basis* involves carrying out a stock take of all items held at regular intervals (often twice a year).

Continuous stock taking is a constant process where selected items are counted on a rotating basis, with all items being checked at least once a year (expensive, desirable or high-turnover items will need to be checked more frequently).

The number of items actually held is recorded on a stock list by the person doing the stock take. An extract from a stock list is shown on the next page; it shows the A4 paper seen in the stock record. The stock list will, of course, contain many items when the stock take has been completed.

stock list as at 9 April 2007					checker H Ramsay		
product code	item description	location	unit size	units counted	stock record balance	discrepancy	checker's initials
P1026	A4 white photocopying paper	row A, bin 6	ream	895	895	nil	HR

checker's signature *H Ramsay*   **Authorised for write-off**

January	Opening stock of 40 units at a cost of £3.00 each
February	Bought 20 units at a cost of £3.60 each
March	Sold 36 units for £6 each
April	Bought 20 units at a cost of £3.75 each
May	Sold 25 units for £6 each

What will be the profit for the period using each stock valuation method?

solution

Note: In the first two methods – FIFO and LIFO – units issued at the same time may be valued at different costs. This is because the quantities received, with their costs, are listed separately and used in a specific order. There may be insufficient units at one cost, eg see the May issue using both FIFO and LIFO methods.

FIFO

STORES LEDGER RECORD

Date	Receipts			Issues			Balance		
2007	Quantity	Cost	Total Cost	Quantity	Cost	Total Cost	Quantity	Cost	Total Cost
		£	£		£	£		£	£
Jan	Balance						40	3.00	120.00
Feb	20	3.60	72.00				40	3.00	120.00
							20	3.60	72.00
							60		192.00
March				36	3.00	108.00	4	3.00	12.00
							20	3.60	72.00
							24		84.00
April	20	3.75	75.00				4	3.00	12.00
							20	3.60	72.00
							20	3.75	75.00
							44		159.00
May				4	3.00	12.00			
				20	3.60	72.00			
				1	3.75	3.75	19	3.75	71.25

Note: In the 'Balance' columns, a new list of stock quantities and costs is started after each receipt or issue. When stock is issued, costs are used from the **top** of the list downwards.

LIFO

STORES LEDGER RECORD

Date	Receipts			Issues			Balance		
2007	Quantity	Cost	Total Cost	Quantity	Cost	Total Cost	Quantity	Cost	Total Cost
		£	£		£	£		£	£
Jan	Balance						40	3.00	120.00
Feb	20	3.60	72.00				40	3.00	120.00
							20	3.60	72.00
							60		192.00
March				20	3.60	72.00			
				16	3.00	48.00	24	3.00	72.00
April	20	3.75	75.00				24	3.00	72.00
							20	3.75	75.00
							44		147.00
May				20	3.75	75.00			
				5	3.00	15.00	19	3.00	57.00

Note: In the 'Balance' columns, a new list of stock quantities and costs is started after each receipt or issue. When stock is issued, costs are used from the **bottom** of the list upwards. However, the new balance list each time must be kept in date order.

AVCO

In this method, each quantity issued is valued at the weighted average cost per unit, and so is the balance in stock. The complete list of different costs does not have to be re-written each time.

STORES LEDGER RECORD

Date	Receipts			Issues			Balance		
2007	Quantity	Cost	Total Cost	Quantity	Cost	Total Cost	Quantity	Cost	Total Cost
		£	£		£	£		£	£
Jan	Balance						40	3.00	120.00
Feb	20	3.60	72.00				40	3.00	120.00
							20	3.60	72.00
							60	3.20	192.00
March				36	3.20	115.20	24	3.20	76.80
April	20	3.75	75.00				24	3.20	76.80
							20	3.75	75.00
							44	3.45	151.80
May				25	3.45	86.25	19	3.45	65.55

Note: Weighted average cost is calculated by dividing the quantity held in stock into the value of the stock. For example, at the end of February, the weighted average cost is £192 ÷ 60 units = £3.20, and at the end of April it is £151.80 ÷ 44 = £3.45.

The closing stock valuations at the end of May 2007 under each method show total cost prices of:

FIFO	£71.25
LIFO	£57.00
AVCO	£65.55

There is quite a difference, and this has come about because different stock methods have been used.

effect on profit

In the example above, the selling price was £6 per unit. The effect on gross profit of using different stock valuations is shown below.

		FIFO	LIFO	AVCO
		£	£	£
Sales: 61 units at £6		366.00	366.00	366.00
Opening stock:	40 units at £3	120.00	120.00	120.00
Purchases:	20 units at £3.60 and 20 units at £3.75	147.00	147.00	147.00
		267.00	267.00	267.00
Less Closing stock: 19 units		71.25	57.00	65.55
Cost of sales		195.75	210.00	201.45
Gross profit = Sales − Cost of sales		170.25	156.00	164.55

Notice that the cost of sales figure in each case is also obtainable by adding up the values in the 'Issues' column. You can also check in each case that, both in Units and in Values:

opening stock + receipts − issues = closing stock

The Case Study shows that in times of rising prices, FIFO produces the highest reported profit, LIFO the lowest, and AVCO between the other two. However, over the life of a business, total profit is the same in total, whichever method is chosen: the profit is allocated to different years depending on which method is used.

The choice of method depends on which method is considered to give the most useful information for management purposes.

ADVANTAGES AND DISADVANTAGES OF FIFO, LIFO AND AVCO

FIFO (first in, first out)

advantages

- it is realistic, ie it assumes that goods are issued in order of receipt
- it is easy to calculate
- stock valuation comprises actual costs at which items have been bought
- the closing stock valuation is close to the most recent costs

disadvantages

- costs at which goods are issued are not necessarily the latest prices
- in times of rising prices, profits will be higher than with other methods (resulting in more tax to pay)
- the method is cumbersome as the list of different costs must be maintained

LIFO (last in, first out)

advantages

- goods are issued at the latest costs
- it is easy to calculate
- in manufacturing, materials are issued at more up-to-date costs, giving a more realistic production cost

disadvantages

- illogical, ie it assumes goods are issued in reverse order from that in which they are received
- the closing stock valuation is not usually at most recent costs
- when stocks are being run down, issues will 'dip into' old stock at out-of-date costs
- may not be acceptable to HM Revenue & Customs for taxation purposes as the method overstates cost of sales and understates profit
- the method is cumbersome as the list of different costs must be maintained

AVCO (weighted average cost)

advantages

- over a number of accounting periods reported profits are smoothed, ie both high and low profits are avoided
- fluctuations in purchase costs are evened out so that issues do not vary greatly
- logical, ie it assumes that identical units, even when purchased at different times, have the same value
- closing stock valuation is close to current market values (in times of rising prices, it will be below current market values)
- the calculations can be computerised more easily than the other methods

disadvantages

- a new weighted average has to be calculated after each receipt, and calculations may be to several decimal places
- issues and stock valuation are usually at costs which never existed
- issues may not be at current costs and, in times of rising prices, will be below current costs

The important point to remember is that a business must adopt a consistent stock valuation policy, ie it should choose one method of finding the cost price, and not change it without good reason. FIFO and AVCO are more commonly used than LIFO; in particular, LIFO usually results in a stock valuation for the final accounts which bears little relationship to recent costs – for this reason it is not favoured by SSAP 9. However, LIFO has the advantage that it gives a more realistic production cost – this is because materials are issued at more up-to-date prices. It is also appropriate to apply LIFO principles when costing materials in a quotation to be given to a potential customer: in times of rising prices you wouldn't want to quote old prices – for example, under FIFO – and then, when the quotation is accepted, find that there is no more of the older-priced materials left.

Now study the table on the next page to consolidate what you have learnt so far.

a comparison of the methods of stock valuation

	FIFO	LIFO	AVCO
method	The costs used for goods sold or issued follow the order in which the goods were received.	The costs used for goods sold or issued are opposite to the order in which the goods were received.	Does not relate issues to any particular batch of goods received, but uses a weighted average cost.
calculation	It is easy to calculate costs because they relate to specific receipts of materials or goods.	It is easy to calculate costs because they relate to specific receipts of materials or goods.	More complex because of the need to calculate weighted average costs.
stock valuation	Stock valuations are based on the most recent costs of materials or goods received.	Stock valuations are based on older costs of materials or goods received.	Weighted average costs are used to value closing stock.
profits and taxation	In times of rising prices this method will result in higher reported profits than the other methods, resulting in more tax being payable. This method is acceptable for tax purposes.	In times of rising prices this method will result in lower reported profits than the other methods. This may not be acceptable for tax purposes.	The weighted average method will smooth out some of the peaks and troughs of profit and loss. This method is acceptable for tax purposes.
administration	Use of this method will mean keeping track of each receipt until the goods are issued or sold.	Use of this method will mean keeping track of each receipt until the goods are issued or sold.	There is no need to track each receipt as a weighted average cost is used. This also means it is easier to computerise the stock records.
cost of sales	In a time of rising prices this method will use older, out of date prices for cost of sales or goods issued.	In a time of rising prices this method will use more up-to-date prices for cost of sales or goods issued.	This method will give an average price for the cost of sales.

CATEGORIES OF STOCK

Statement of Standard Accounting Practice No 9 requires that, in calculating the lower of cost and net realisable value, note should be taken of:

–   separate items of stock, or

–   groups of similar items

This means that the stock valuation 'rule' must be applied to each separate item of stock, or each group or category of similar stocks. The total cost cannot be compared with the total net realisable value, as is shown by the Case Study which follows.

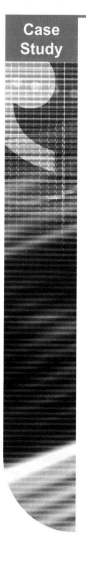

Case Study

PAINT AND WALLPAPER SUPPLIES: VALUING YEAR-END STOCKS

situation

The year-end stocks for the two main groups of stock held by the business Paint and Wallpaper Supplies are found to be:

	Cost	Net realisable value
	£	£
Paints	2,500	2,300
Wallpapers	5,000	7,500
	7,500	9,800

How will the stock be valued for the year-end accounts?

solution

The correct stock valuation is £7,300, which takes the 'lower of cost and net realisable value' for each group of stock, ie

	£
Paints (at net realisable value)	2,300
Wallpapers (at cost)	5,000
	7,300

You will also note that this valuation is the lowest possible choice, indicating that stock valuation follows the *prudence concept* of accounting.

BLUE JEANS LIMITED:
BOOK-KEEPING FOR MATERIALS COSTS

situation

Blue Jeans Limited manufactures and sells denim jeans and jackets. The company uses the first in, first out (FIFO) method for valuing issues of materials to production and stocks of materials.

The company has been very busy in recent weeks and, as a consequence, some of the accounting records are not up-to-date. The following stores ledger record has not been completed:

STORES LEDGER RECORD

Product: Blue denim

	Receipts			Issues			Balance	
Date 2007	Quantity metres	Cost per metre £	Total Cost £	Quantity metres	Cost per metre £	Total Cost £	Quantity metres	Total Cost £
Balance at 1 Oct							20,000	10,000
11 Oct	10,000	0.60	6,000				30,000	16,000
14 Oct				25,000				
19 Oct	20,000	0.70	14,000					
25 Oct				20,000				

All issues of blue denim are for the manufacture of blue jeans. The following cost accounting codes are used to record material costs:

code number	description
2000	stock of blue denim
2200	work-in-progress – blue jeans
4000	creditors/purchases ledger control

As an accounts assistant at Blue Jeans Limited, you are asked to complete the stores ledger record and to fill in the table (below) to record separately the two purchases and two issues of blue denim in the cost accounting records.

2007	Code	Debit	Credit
11 October	2000		
11 October	4000		
14 October	2000		
14 October	2200		
19 October	2000		
19 October	4000		
25 October	2000		
25 October	2200		

solution

The stores ledger record is completed as shown on the next page.

Note that there may be a need to calculate the balance from more than one receipt cost. For example, on 11 October, the balance is made up of:

			£
20,000	metres at £0.50 per metre	=	10,000
10,000	metres at £0.60 per metre	=	6,000
30,000	metres	=	16,000

Similarly, on 19 October, the balance is made up of:

			£
5,000	metres at £0.60 per metre	=	3,000
20,000	metres at £0.70 per metre	=	14,000
25,000		=	17,000

STORES LEDGER RECORD

Product: **Blue denim**

Date 2007	Receipts			Issues			Balance	
	Quantity metres	Cost per metre £	Total Cost £	Quantity metres	Cost per metre £	Total Cost £	Quantity metres	Total Cost £
Balance at 1 Oct							20,000	10,000
11 Oct	10,000	0.60	6,000				30,000	16,000*
14 Oct				25,000	20,000 x 0.50 5,000 x 0.60	10,000 3,000 13,000	5,000	3,000
19 Oct	20,000	0.70	14,000				25,000	17,000**
25 Oct				20,000	5,000 x 0.60 15,000 x 0.70	3,000 10,500 13,500	5,000	3,500

* £10,000 + £6,000   ** £3,000 + £14,000

The cost book-keeping entries are:

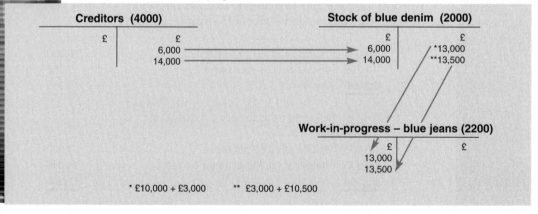

Creditors (4000)		Stock of blue denim (2000)	
£	£ 6,000 14,000	£ 6,000 14,000	£ *13,000 **13,500

Work-in-progress – blue jeans (2200)

£ 13,000 13,500	£

* £10,000 + £3,000   ** £3,000 + £10,500

The cost book-keeping entries are recorded on the table as follows:

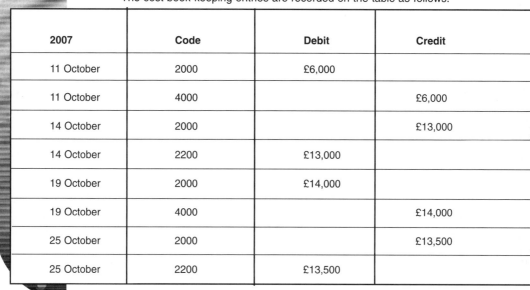

2007	Code	Debit	Credit
11 October	2000	£6,000	
11 October	4000		£6,000
14 October	2000		£13,000
14 October	2200	£13,000	
19 October	2000	£14,000	
19 October	4000		£14,000
25 October	2000		£13,500
25 October	2200	£13,500	

Chapter Summary

- Businesses and other organisations hold stocks of raw materials and components bought for production, products bought for resale, and service items bought for use within the business.

- Two important stock costs are the ordering cost and the stock holding cost.

- Materials purchases can be made using techniques such as:
  - the level method of re-ordering
  - Economic Order Quantity (EOQ)
  - Just-In-Time (JIT)

- The level of stock is recorded on a stock record, which also indicates
  - the level at which new stock should be ordered
  - the quantity of stock that should be re-ordered

- Stock levels of materials are monitored regularly by means of stock taking; stock reconciliation notes any discrepancies and reports them for further investigation.

- Stock valuation is normally made *at the lower of cost and net realisable value* (SSAP 9).

- Stock valuation methods include:
  - FIFO (first in, first out)
  - LIFO (last in, first out)
  - AVCO (weighted average cost)
  - standard cost
  - replacement cost

- For a manufacturer, cost comprises the direct manufacturing costs of materials, labour and expenses, together with the production overheads which bring the product to its present location or condition.

- Cost book-keeping entries are made to record stock transactions such as:
  - the purchase of materials on credit from suppliers
  - the issue of materials to work-in-progress/part-finished goods

Key Terms

materials	the cost of: - raw materials and components used in production - products bought for resale - service items bought for use within the business
level method of re-ordering	the re-ordering of materials in fixed quantities
Economic Order Quantity (EOQ)	a balance between ordering costs and stock holding costs; calculated by the formula: $$\sqrt{\dfrac{2 \times \text{annual usage} \times \text{ordering cost}}{\text{stock holding cost}}}$$
Just-In-Time (JIT)	the process of delivering goods in the right quantities, in the right place, just-in-time
stock record	record held for each stock item which shows receipts of supplies and sales (or issues to production)
stock taking	the process of counting physical stock on hand
stock reconciliation	comparison of the physical stock on hand with the stock record balance and identification of the reason(s) for discrepancies
stock value	number of items held x stock valuation per item

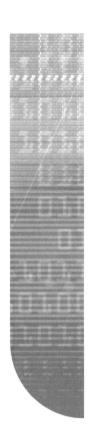

cost	the amount it cost to buy the stock (including additional costs to bring the product to its present location or condition)
net realisable value	selling price (less any extra costs, such as selling and distribution)
FIFO	'First in, first out' method of attaching a value to each issue of materials or goods from stores, using the oldest cost prices first
LIFO	'Last in, first out' method of attaching a value to each issue of materials or goods from stores, using most recent cost prices first
AVCO	'Average cost' method of attaching a value to each issue of materials or goods from stores, using a weighted average of the cost prices of all items in stock at the date of issue
stores ledger record (stock card)	method of recording stock data in order to ascertain the cost at which stocks of materials are issued, and to ascertain a valuation of stock
cost book-keeping	double-entry system to record costing transactions; uses the principles of double-entry book-keeping

Student Activities

2.1 Calculate, for stock items D and E, the re-order stock level and the re-order quantity to replenish stock levels to the maximum level, from the following information:

- daily usage of D = 3 units, of E = 4 units

- total stock should never exceed 95 days' usage

- 10 days' stock should always be held

- there is space available in the store for 350 units of each item of stock

- lead time is 7 days

2.2 **(a)** Prepare a stock record from the following information:

- *product:* A4 Yellow Card, code A4/Y3, location row 7, bin 5
- *units:* reams
- *maximum stock level:* 35 days' usage
- *daily usage:* 3 units
- *lead time:* 10 days
- *minimum stock level:* 12 days' stock
- *opening balance on 1 May 2007:* 84 reams

Note: a blank stock record, which may be photocopied, is provided in the Appendix.

(b) Calculate maximum, minimum and re-order levels of stock, together with re-order quantity (to replenish stock to the maximum level)

(c) Enter the following materials requisitions for May 2007 on the stock record remembering to re-order when necessary and to show the order arriving ten days later (Goods Received Note 4507):

4 May	Materials Requisition 184	18 reams
6 May	Materials Requisition 187	20 reams
10 May	Materials Requisition 188	10 reams
17 May	Materials Requisition 394	20 reams
20 May	Materials Requisition 401	11 reams
26 May	Materials Requisition 422	6 reams

2.3 Complete the following sentences:

(a) Stock levels and movements are recorded on a ....

(b) A person carrying out a stock check will record the stock on a ....

(c) The process of comparing stock on the shelves with stock in the records is known as

....

(d) The usual basis for stock valuation is at the lower of .... and ....

....

2.4   From the following information prepare stores ledger records for product X using:

(a) FIFO

(b) LIFO

(c) AVCO

- 20 units of the product are bought in January 2007 at a cost of £3 each

- 10 units are bought in February at a cost of £3.50 each

- 8 units are sold in March

- 10 units are bought in April at a cost of £4.00 each

- 16 units are sold in May

Notes:

- a blank stores ledger record, which may be photocopied, is provided in the Appendix

- where appropriate, work to two decimal places

2.5   XY Limited is formed on 1 January 2007 and, at the end of its first half-year of trading, the stores ledger records show the following:

2007	TYPE X		TYPE Y	
	Receipts (units)	**Issues (units)**	**Receipts (units)**	**Issues (units)**
January	100 at £4.00		200 at £10.00	
February		80	100 at £9.50	
March	140 at £4.20			240
April	100 at £3.80		100 at £10.50	
May		140	140 at £10.00	
June	80 at £4.50			100

At 30 June 2007, the net realisable value of each type of stock is:

type X	£1,750
type Y	£1,950
	£3,700

You are to:

- Complete stores ledger records for products X and Y using (a) FIFO, (b) LIFO, (c) AVCO.

- The business has decided to use the FIFO method. Show the amount at which its stocks should be valued on 30 June 2007 in order to comply with standard accounting practice.

Notes:

- a blank stores ledger record, which may be photocopied, is provided in the Appendix

- where appropriate, work to two decimal places

2.6 Breeden Bakery Limited makes 'homestyle' cakes which are sold to supermarket chains.

The company uses the first in, first out (FIFO) method for valuing issues of materials to production and stocks of materials.

As an accounts assistant at Breeden Bakery you have been given the following tasks.

Task 1

Complete the following stores ledger record for wholewheat flour for May 2007:

STORES LEDGER RECORD

Product: Wholewheat flour

Date	Receipts			Issues			Balance	
	Quantity kgs	Cost per kg	Total Cost	Quantity kgs	Cost per kg	Total Cost	Quantity kgs	Total Cost
2007		£	£		£	£		£
Balance at 1 May							10,000	2,500
6 May	20,000	0.30	6,000				30,000	8,500
10 May				20,000				
17 May	10,000	0.35	3,500					
20 May				15,000				

Task 2

All issues of wholewheat flour are for the manufacture of fruit cakes. The following cost accounting codes are used to record materials costs:

code number	description
3000	stock of wholewheat flour
3300	work-in-progress – fruit cakes
5000	creditors/purchases ledger control

Complete the table below to record separately the two purchases and two issues of wholewheat flour in the cost accounting records.

2007	Code	Debit	Credit
6 May	3000		
6 May	5000		
10 May	3000		
10 May	3300		
17 May	3000		
17 May	5000		
20 May	3000		
20 May	3300		

3 Labour costs

this chapter covers . . .

In this chapter we explain:

- *the factors that affect labour costs*
- *the ways in which the direct labour employees of a business or organisation can be remunerated*
- *how payroll information is gathered*
- *the advantages and disadvantages of different labour remuneration methods*
- *overtime and idle time*
- *the book-keeping entries for labour costs*

PERFORMANCE CRITERIA COVERED

unit 6: RECORDING AND ANALYSING COSTS AND REVENUES

element 6.1

record and analyse information relating to direct costs and revenues

A   *identify direct costs in accordance with the organisation's costing procedures*

B   *record and analyse information relating to direct costs*

C   *calculate direct costs in accordance with the organisation's policies and procedures*

E   *resolve or refer queries to the appropriate person*

ACCOUNTING FOR LABOUR COSTS

We saw in Chapter 1 how costs may be classified as materials costs, labour costs and expenses. All businesses incur labour costs: the costs of wages and salaries of all their employees.

factors that affect labour costs

There are many factors that need to be considered by a business when deciding how much to pay employees. The starting point will always be the amount that is paid by other businesses in the area for similar grades of employees but, at the same time, the wider economic implications of supply and demand will affect wage rates.

The factors to consider include:

- wage rates paid by other local businesses

- comparisons with national average wage rates

- the national minimum wage rate imposed by government

- any government incentives to take on additional employees, such as young people or the long-term unemployed

- local employment conditions – high unemployment in the area will drive down wage rates; conversely low unemployment, and especially a shortage of skilled labour, will increase wage rates

- housing and transport costs in the locality

- the impact of interest rate changes, and exchange rates (eg against the euro) on business confidence

- for a new business, it might be prudent to choose to locate in an area of high unemployment – in addition to lower wage rates, there may be government incentives in the form of reduced rents and rates, training and other grants

Before taking on labour, a business must decide how to calculate gross pay for its employees. The methods of labour remuneration are looked at in detail on the next page.

Earnings are usually calculated according to time worked or work done, or a combination of both.

From time-to-time, employees will expect their pay rates to be reviewed and then, most probably, increased. Usually such a process takes place each year when wage rates are negotiated. In the negotiations, both the employer and the representatives of the employees will take into account such things as:

- the rise in the cost of living, for example, as measured by the Retail Price Index (RPI)

- the overall employment situation

- the profitability of the business – can it afford to pay increased wage rates?

While the employer will be seeking a package of measures that gives the business a more efficient workforce, employees will be looking for higher wages together with enhanced benefits.

LABOUR REMUNERATION

Direct labour cost is the wages paid to those who work on a production line, are involved in assembly, or are involved in the output of a service business.

The three main methods of direct labour remuneration are:

time rate Time rate (sometimes known as a day rate) is where the employee is paid on the basis of time spent at work. Overtime may be paid for hours worked beyond a standard number of hours, or for work carried out on days which are not part of the working week, eg Saturdays or Sundays. Overtime is often paid at rates such as 'time-and-a-quarter', 'time-and-a-half', or even 'double-time'.

'Time-and-a-half', for example, means that 1.5 times the basic hourly rate is paid.

piecework rate The employee is paid an agreed sum for each task carried out or for each unit of output completed.

In some cases, employees may have a guaranteed minimum wage.

bonus system The employee is paid a time rate and then receives a bonus if output is better than expected. Such systems are often linked into standard costing – covered in your later studies – where the quantity of work that can be achieved at a standard performance in an hour (a standard hour) is estimated; the bonus is then expressed as an agreed percentage of the standard hours saved.

Bonus systems base employees' earnings on a combination of time taken and work done.

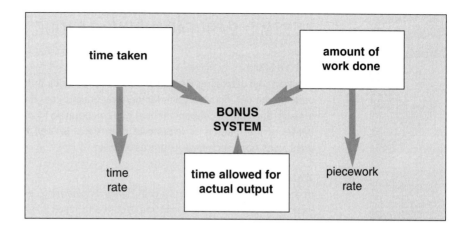

Most other employees, eg factory supervisors, sales staff, office staff, are usually paid on a weekly or monthly basis. Such wages and salaries – classed as indirect labour costs – may be increased by bonus payments; for example, a production bonus for factory supervisors, commissions for sales staff, a profit-sharing scheme for all employees.

There are many variations on the three methods outlined above and, indeed, changing patterns of employment create different remuneration methods from those that would have been the norm just a few years ago. For example, the contracting out of many business support services – such as cleaning, security, computers – means that the costing of such services by the provider may incorporate time rates and bonus systems whereas previously the employees would have been paid on a weekly or monthly basis.

In order to calculate gross wages, information about hours worked and/or work done must be recorded. The documents used include:

*   *time sheets,* where employees record the hours they have worked
*   *clock cards*, where employees 'clock in' at the start of work, and 'clock out' at the end – these are often computerised
*   *piecework tickets,* completed by employees who work on a batch of output
*   *job cards,* where each employee records the amount of time spent on each job
*   *route cards* – which are used to follow a product through the production process – on which employees record the amount of time they spend working on the product
*   *computer cards* – 'swipe' cards which link direct into the computerised payroll are increasingly being used by employers to record attendance

Case Study

WESTMID MANUFACTURING: LABOUR REMUNERATION

situation

Westmid Manufacturing Company has three factories in the West Midlands making parts for the car industry. Each factory was bought from the previous owners and, as a result, each has a different method for remunerating its direct labour workforce. The details of the method of remuneration in each factory, together with data on two employees from each factory, are as follows:

WALSALL FACTORY

In this factory, which is involved in heavy engineering, employees are paid on the basis of a time rate. Employees are required to 'clock in' and 'clock out' each day.

John Brown is a machine operator and his clock card for last week shows that he worked 39 hours; his hourly rate of pay is £8 per hour.

Stefan Wozniak is a skilled lathe operator and his clock card shows that he worked 42 hours; his hourly rate of pay is £10 per hour, with overtime for hours worked beyond 40 hours at 'time-and-a-half'.

DUDLEY FACTORY

This factory operates a number of light engineering production lines making car components such as windscreen wiper blades, headlamp surrounds, interior mirrors etc. The production line employees are all paid on a piecework basis; however, each employee receives a guaranteed time rate which is paid if the piecework earnings are less than the time rate. This may happen if, for example, there are machine breakdowns and the production line has to be halted.

Tracey Johnson works on the line making headlamp surrounds. For each one that passes through her part of the process, she is paid 30p; her guaranteed time rate is 37 hours each week at £6 per hour. Last week's production records show that she processed 870 units.

Pete Bronyah is on the line which makes interior mirrors. For his part of the process he receives £1.00 for each one, with a guaranteed time rate of 37 hours at £6 per hour. Last week there was a machine failure and he was only able to process 150 units.

WOLVERHAMPTON FACTORY

In this factory a number of engineering production lines are operated. The direct labour force is paid on a time rate basis, but a bonus is paid if work can be completed faster than the standard performance. Thus a standard time allowance is given for each task and, if it can be completed in less time, a bonus is paid: the bonus in this factory is for the savings achieved to be shared equally between employer and employee. Wages are, therefore, paid on the following basis: time rate + 50% of (time saved x time rate). If no bonus is due, then the time rate applies.

Martin Lee worked a 38 hour work last week; his time rate is £10 per hour. He is allowed a standard time of 30 minutes to carry out his work on each unit of production; last week he completed 71 units.

Sara King has a time rate of £11 per hour; last week she worked 40 hours. She is allowed a standard time of 15 minutes to carry out her work on each unit of production; last week she completed 184 units.

What were the gross earnings of each employee?

solution

WALSALL FACTORY

John Brown	39 hours x £8.00 per hour	=	£312.00
Stefan Wozniak	40 hours x £10.00 per hour = £400		
	2 hours x £15.00 per hour = £30	=	£430.00

DUDLEY FACTORY

Tracey Johnson	Piecework rate, 870 units x 30p per unit	=	£261.00
	Guaranteed time rate, 37 hours x £6.00 per hour =		£222.00
	Therefore piecework rate of £261.00 is paid.		

Pete Bronyah	Piecework rate, 150 units x £1.00 per unit	=	£150.00
	Guaranteed time rate, 37 hours x £6.00 per hour =		£222.00
	Therefore guaranteed time rate of £222.00 is paid.		

WOLVERHAMPTON FACTORY

Martin Lee	Time rate, 38 hours x £10.00 per hour	=	£380.00
	Bonus, time allowed 71 units x 30 minutes each = 35 hours 30 minutes		
	Therefore no time saved, so no bonus payable.		
	Time rate of £380 paid.		

Sara King	Time rate, 40 hours x £11.00 per hour	=	£440.00
	Bonus, time allowed 184 x 15 minutes each = 46 hours		
	Therefore time saved is 6 hours		
	Bonus is 50% of (6 hours x £11.00)	=	£33.00
	Therefore wages are £440.00 + £33.00	=	£473.00

The Case Study illustrates some of the direct labour remuneration methods in use, however it should be appreciated that there are many variations on these to be found.

DIRECT LABOUR REMUNERATION METHODS: ADVANTAGES AND DISADVANTAGES

time rate

Time rate is often used where it is difficult to measure output, and where quality is more important than quantity. Variations include a high time rate, used to motivate employees where a higher standard of work is required.

advantages:
- easy to understand and to calculate
- no requirement to establish time allowances and piecework rates
- the employee receives a regular wage, unaffected by fluctuations in output
- the employer pays a regular amount, making planning for cash flows easier
- can be used for all direct labour employees
- quality of the finished product does not suffer as a result of hurried work

disadvantages:
- both efficient and inefficient employees receive the same wage
- no incentive is given to employees to work harder
- slower working will not affect basic wage, but may lead to overtime
- more supervisors are needed to ensure that output is maintained

piecework rate

Piecework rate is used where the quantity of output is important, and there is less emphasis on quality. Variations include:

- piecework with guaranteed time rate, which ensures that employees are paid if production is stopped through no fault of their own, eg machine breakdown, or shortage of materials

- differential piecework system, where a higher rate is paid for all output beyond a certain level, eg 50p per unit for the first 100 units each day, then 60p per unit thereafter; used to motivate employees to produce more than a basic level of output

- attendance allowances, paid to encourage employees on piecework to attend each day, thus ensuring that the production-line can be staffed and operated every working day *advantages:*

- payment of wages is linked directly to output
- more efficient workers earn more than those who are less efficient
- work is done quicker and less time is wasted

disadvantages:

- not suitable for all direct labour employees
- pay is reduced if there are production problems, eg machine breakdown or shortage of materials
- quality of the finished product may be low
- more inspectors may be needed
- control systems needed to check the amount produced by each worker
- more complex pay calculations
- may be difficulty in agreeing piecework rates with employees
- the employer cannot plan ahead for wages so easily, as they may be irregular amounts

bonus systems

Bonus systems are used to encourage employees to be more efficient in an environment where the work is not so repetitive. Variations include an accelerating premium bonus – which is an increased bonus paid for higher levels of output, and group bonuses paid to groups of employees who achieve increased output – the group could be as large as the entire workforce of a large company, or as small as a work team of two or three people.

advantages:

- wages linked to output, but minimum wage is guaranteed each week
- work is done quicker and less time is wasted
- more efficient workers earn more
- a bonus system can often be applied to the entire workforce

disadvantages:

- bonus is not paid if circumstances beyond employee's control prevent work, eg machine breakdown or shortage of materials
- quality of finished product may be low
- more inspectors may be needed and additional control procedures
- pay calculations may be more complex
- there may be difficulty in agreeing bonus rates with employees

- group bonus schemes may cause conflict within the group, if some workers consider that others are working too slowly

qualities of a good labour remuneration scheme

These include:

- reward should be related to effort and fair to all staff
- the scheme should be easy to manage and administer, and cheap and efficient to run
- it should be easy for employees to understand how pay is calculated
- payment should be made at regular intervals and soon after the event, eg employees on piecework should be paid in the week after the production has been achieved
- the principles of the scheme should remain constant, but there should be flexibility to deal with changes in production techniques

summary

The three main methods of remuneration, together with some alternative systems, are summarised in the table on the next page.

As an accounts assistant, always remember that payroll information is confidential and any queries should be referred to the appropriate person – for example, the payroll manager, or the accounts supervisor.

OVERTIME AND IDLE TIME

In Chapter 1 we divided labour costs between:

- **direct costs,** labour costs of production-line employees
- **indirect costs,** labour costs of other employees, such as supervisors, office staff, etc

Whilst this distinction appears clear enough, there are times when a proportion of the labour costs of production-line employees is classed as an indirect cost (rather than a direct cost) and is included amongst the overheads of the business. This is done if part of the cost of wages of the direct workers cannot be linked to specific work.

overtime payments

When production-line employees work overtime they are usually paid at a rate above the time rate. For example, overtime might be paid at 'time-and-a-half'; thus an employee with a time rate of £8 an hour will be paid overtime at £12 an hour. The additional £4 per hour is called **overtime premium**. For

continued on page 82

methods of remuneration – a summary

	TIME RATE	PIECEWORK RATE	BONUS SYSTEM
situation	This system is used where it is difficult to measure the quantity of output and where quality is more important than volume of output.	This system is used where the work is repetitive and quantity of output is more important than quality.	This system is used to motivate employees, where the work is not so repetitive as in piecework but is measurable.
gross pay calculation	Hours worked x rate per hour This is easy to calculate and understand.	Number of items produced x rate per item This is easy to calculate and understand.	Basic pay + proportion of the time saved Time saved is the difference between time allowed and time taken to do a task. More complex to calculate and understand.
motivation	Pay is not linked to output and therefore there is no incentive to work hard. Slower workers may get paid overtime at higher rates.	Pay is related directly to output. There is a direct incentive to work as the amount of output determines the amount paid.	There is some incentive to work in order to earn a bonus as well as basic pay.
quality of output	There is no pressure on time and so quality should be maintained.	The fact that pay is related to output means it is important that quality standards of output are met.	The link between pay and output means that the quality of output needs to be checked.
control	It is important that the volume and quality of output is maintained.	It is important that the volume and quality of output is maintained.	It is important that the volume and quality of output is maintained.
administration	There is no need to set time allowances for output.	There is a need to set time allowances for work done and to keep these up to date.	There is a need to set time allowances for work done and to keep these up to date.
payment to employees	A regular amount is earned by the employee.	The amount earned by the employee varies with the output the employee produces.	There is some regular income but pay can be increased by additional effort.
ALTERNATIVE SYSTEMS	**High day rate** – employees are paid a higher than average rate per hour but agree to produce a given amount of output at a given quality.	**Attendance allowance** – to ensure employees turn up. **Guaranteed day rate** – to give employees a minimum payment. **Differential piecework** – to pay efficient workers more for output beyond a given level of output, ie an extra amount per unit.	**Group bonus schemes** – used where employees work as a group. This can include all workers, eg cleaners. This may create problems as the most efficient workers may be held back by the less efficient workers.

normal cost accounting purposes, any overtime worked is charged at £8 an hour to direct labour, and £4 an hour to indirect labour.

Example:

A group of employees on a production line have a working week consisting of 40 hours each. Anything over that time is paid at time-and-a-half. One employee has worked 43 hours during the week at a normal rate of £8.

- Direct wages cost is 43 hours at £8 = £344
- Overtime premium is 3 hours at £4 (half of £8) = £12, which is charged to indirect labour

In this way, the cost of overtime is spread across all output and is not charged solely to the output being worked on during the overtime period. As another issue, management will wish to know why there was the need to work overtime, and will seek to control such an increase in labour costs.

However, where a customer requests overtime to be worked to get a rush job completed, then the full overtime rate (£12 an hour in the above example) is charged as direct labour, and passed on as a cost to the customer.

Other additional payments made to employees – such as a bonus – will be treated in a similar way to overtime and will normally be treated as an indirect labour cost.

idle time

Idle time occurs when production is stopped through no fault of the production-line employees – for example, a machine breakdown, or a shortage of materials. Employees paid under a piecework or a bonus system will receive time rate for the period of the stoppage. Such wages costs are normally charged to overheads as indirect labour.

Similarly, time spent by direct workers on non-productive work would also usually be treated as an overhead.

BOOK-KEEPING FOR LABOUR COSTS

In this section we look at the cost book-keeping entries to record labour costs – the transfer of labour costs to work-in-progress and to overheads. These entries form part of the book-keeping system for costing; Chapter 7 looks in detail at an integrated book-keeping system.

A **wages control account** – which may also include salaries – is used to charge labour costs to the various cost centres of a business or organisation.

In this way:

- direct labour costs are charged to work-in-progress
- indirect labour costs are charged to production overheads
- administration labour costs are charged to non-production overheads

The cost book-keeping entries are:

- **transfer of direct labour costs to work-in-progress**
  - debit work-in-progress account
  - credit wages control account

- **transfer of indirect labour costs to production overheads**
  - debit production overheads account
  - credit wages control account

- **transfer of administration labour costs to non-production overheads**
  - debit non-production overheads account, eg administration
  - credit wages control account

The cost book-keeping entries are shown diagrammatically as follows:

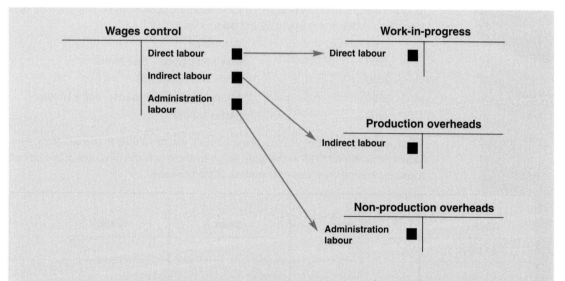

Note: Here all of the labour costs have been transferred to work-in-progress and overheads. From time-to-time, however, some part of labour costs may relate to capital expenditure (see page 94) – for example, own workforce used to build an extension to the premises; here the book-keeping entries for the relevant labour costs are:
- debit premises account (or relevant capital expenditure account)
- credit wages control account

BLUE JEANS LIMITED: BOOK-KEEPING FOR LABOUR COSTS

situation

Blue Jeans Limited manufactures and sells denim jeans and jackets. The payroll for the week ended 21 May 2007 has been completed, with the following amounts to pay:

		£
•	net wages to be paid to employees	5,000
•	income tax and National Insurance Contributions (NIC) to be paid to HM Revenue & Customs	1,000
•	pension contributions to be paid to the pension fund	500
	TOTAL PAYROLL FOR THE WEEK	6,500

The total payroll for the week is analysed as:

		£
•	direct labour costs	3,500
•	indirect labour costs	2,000
•	administration labour costs	1,000
		6,500

All of the direct labour costs are for the manufacture of blue jeans. The following cost accounting codes are in use to record labour costs:

code number	description
2200	work-in-progress – blue jeans
2400	production overheads
2600	non-production overheads – administration
4200	wages control

As an accounts assistant at Blue Jeans Limited, you are asked to prepare the wages control account and to fill in the table below to show how the total cost of the payroll is split between the various cost centres of the business.

2007	Code	Debit	Credit
21 May	2200		
21 May	4200		
21 May	2400		
21 May	4200		
21 May	2600		
21 May	4200		

solution

Wages control account is prepared as follows:

Dr		Wages Control Account		Cr
	£			£
Cash/bank (net wages)	5,000	Work-in-progress (direct labour)		3,500
HM Revenue & Customs		Production overheads		
(income tax and NIC)	1,000	(indirect labour)		2,000
Pension contributions	500	Non-production overheads		
		(administration)		1,000
	6,500			6,500

The cost book-keeping entries are:

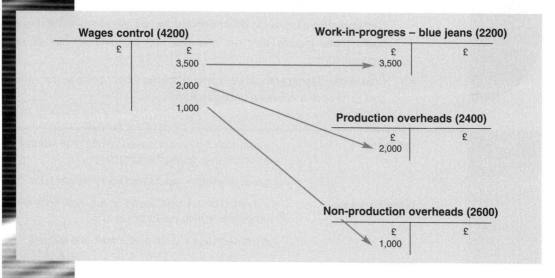

These are recorded on the table as follows:

2007	Code	Debit	Credit
21 May	2200	£3,500	
21 May	4200		£3,500
21 May	2400	£2,000	
21 May	4200		£2,000
21 May	2600	£1,000	
21 May	4200		£1,000

In this way, the total cost of the payroll is split between the various cost centres of the business.

Chapter Summary

- Labour costs are incurred in every kind of business and are influenced by levels of wages and by the method of remuneration.

- Levels of wage rates paid to employees are influenced by a number of factors including the rates paid by similar local businesses, compulsory minimum rates and national averages.

- The main methods of remuneration are based either on time or amounts of work done or on a combination of both.

- Different methods of remuneration have advantages and disadvantages for the employer and the employee. The employer needs to control the cost of wages, but also to motivate employees to produce work of suitable quality within a reasonable time.

- A good remuneration scheme should be fair, easy to understand and efficiently managed.

- Certain wages costs of the direct workers may be classed as indirect labour costs: these include overtime premium and payment for idle or non-productive time.

- Cost book-keeping entries are made to charge labour costs to the various cost centres of a business or organisation.

Key Terms

time rate	a method of payment based on the time worked by an employee, giving the formula: gross earnings = hours worked x rate per hour
piecework rate	a method of payment based on the work done by an employee, giving the formula: gross earnings = units produced x rate per unit
bonus system	a method of payment in which an employee may earn a bonus by completing work in less time than the time allowed – usually the bonus is calculated as a share of the hours saved, multiplied by the rate per hour
standard hour	the quantity of work that can be achieved by one worker in one hour, at a standard level of performance
time sheet	method by which employees record the hours they have worked
clock card	where employees 'clock in' at the start of work, and 'clock out' at the end
piecework ticket	documentation completed by employees who work on a batch of output
job card	documentation completed by employees which records the amount of time spent on each job

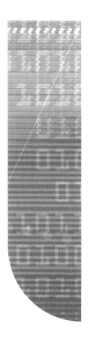

route card	documentation which follows a product through the production process – employees record the amount of time they spend working on the product
overtime premium	the additional pay above normal rates which is paid to employees working overtime, for example, the premium part of 'time-and-a-half' is the extra 'half' of the hourly rate
idle time	time during which work is stopped, due to reasons such as machine breakdown or shortage of materials; employees usually receive time rate for idle time, and the cost is normally classified as an indirect cost
wages control account	used to charge labour costs to the various cost centres:

– direct labour to work-in-progress

– indirect labour to production overheads

– administration labour to non-production overhead

Student Activities

3.1 A manufacturing business pays its production workers on a time rate basis. A bonus is paid where production is completed faster than the standard hour output; the bonus is paid at half of the time rate for production time saved. How much will each of the following employees earn for the week?

Employee	Time rate	Hours worked	Standard hour output	Actual production
N Ball	£8.00 per hour	35	30 units	1,010 units
T Smith	£9.00 per hour	37	40 units	1,560 units
L Lewis	£10.00 per hour	40	20 units	855 units
M Wilson	£7.00 per hour	38	24 units	940 units

3.2 Harrison & Company is a manufacturing business. Currently it pays its production-line workers on a time rate basis. Recently the employee representatives have approached the management of the company with a view to seeking alternative methods of remuneration. Suggestions have been made that either a piecework system, or a time rate with a production bonus system would be more appropriate.

3.8 Breeden Bakery Limited makes 'homestyle' cakes which are sold to supermarket chains. The payroll for the week ended 26 March 2007 has been completed, with the following amounts to pay:

	£
• net wages to be paid to employees	7,500
• income tax and National Insurance Contributions (NIC) to be paid to HM Revenue & Customs	1,450
• pension contributions to be paid to the pension fund	750
TOTAL PAYROLL FOR THE WEEK	9,700

The total payroll for the week is analysed as:

	£
• direct labour costs	6,500
• indirect labour costs	2,700
• administration labour costs	500
	9,700

As an accounts assistant at Breedon Bakery you have been given the following tasks:

Task 1

Prepare wages control account for the week ended 26 March 2007:

Dr	Wages Control Account		Cr
	£		£

Task 2

All of the direct labour costs are for the manufacture of fruit cakes. The following cost accounting codes are in use to record labour costs:

code number	description
3300	work-in-progress – fruit cakes
3500	production overheads
3700	non-production overheads – administration
5200	wages control

Complete the table below to show how the total cost of the payroll is split between the various cost centres of the business.

2007	Code	Debit	Credit
26 March	3300		
26 March	5200		
26 March	3500		
26 March	5200		
26 March	3700		
26 March	5200		

3.9 Icod Limited manufactures golf clubs. The following data relates to the production of its 'Mulligan' brand of clubs for October 2007:

Total direct labour hours worked	16,000 hours
Normal time hours	14,400 hours
Overtime hours	1,600 hours
Normal time rate per hour	£8 per hour
Overtime premium per hour	£4 per hour

In the company's cost book-keeping system all direct labour overtime payments are included in direct costs.

The following cost accounting codes are in use to record labour costs:

code number	description
1500	work-in-progress – 'Mulligan' clubs
5000	wages control

You are to:

• calculate the total cost of direct labour for October

• show the cost book-keeping entries, together with account codes, in order to transfer the direct labour costs to work-in-progress

4 Expenses

In this chapter we examine:

- *expenses as an element of cost*
- *the distinction between capital expenditure and revenue expenditure*
- *the distinction between direct expenses and indirect expenses*
- *the book-keeping entries for expenses*
- *the nature and behaviour of fixed, semi-variable and variable costs*

PERFORMANCE CRITERIA COVERED

unit 6: RECORDING AND ANALYSING COSTS AND REVENUES

element 6.1

record and analyse information relating to direct costs and revenues

A   *identify direct costs in accordance with the organisation's costing procedures*

B   *record and analyse information relating to direct costs*

C   *calculate direct costs in accordance with the organisation's policies and procedures*

E   *resolve or refer queries to the appropriate person*

EXPENSES – AN ELEMENT OF COST

The third main element of cost is that of expenses, ie any cost that cannot be classified as materials or labour. Expenses include items such as rent, rates, telephone, lighting, heating, royalties paid to the designer of a product, special items bought in for a particular product, etc.

It is important that expenses are categorised correctly in order that costs can be calculated accurately and accounting statements can show a true representation of the state of the business. To achieve this, as shown by the diagram below, we need to distinguish between:

- capital expenditure and revenue expenditure
- direct expenses and indirect expenses
- fixed costs and variable costs

Note that both direct and indirect expenses can be either fixed or variable in nature – see page 100.

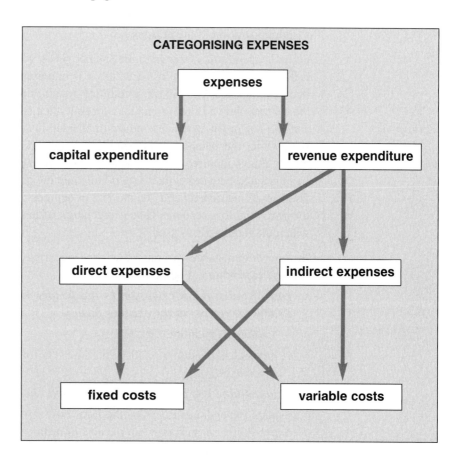

CAPITAL EXPENDITURE AND REVENUE EXPENDITURE

Capital expenditure can be defined as *expenditure incurred on the purchase, alteration or improvement of fixed assets.* For example, the purchase of a car for use in the business is capital expenditure. Included in capital expenditure are costs such as:

* delivery of fixed assets

* installation of fixed assets

* improvement (but not repair) of fixed assets

* legal costs of buying property

Revenue expenditure is *expenditure incurred on running costs.* For example, the cost of petrol or diesel for the car (above) is revenue expenditure. Included in revenue expenditure are the running costs of:

* maintenance and repair of fixed assets

* making, selling and distributing the goods or products in which the business trades

* administration of the business

Capital expenditure is shown in the balance sheet, while revenue expenditure is a cost in the profit and loss account. It is important to classify these types of expenditure correctly in the accounting system. For example, if the cost of the car was shown in profit and loss account, then costs would be overstated and the net profit would be reduced considerably, or a net loss recorded; meanwhile, the balance sheet would not show the car as a fixed asset – clearly this is incorrect as the business owns the asset. Note, however, that there is a link between capital expenditure and the profit and loss account: as fixed assets are depreciated, the amount of depreciation is shown as a cost in the profit and loss account. Thus depreciation relates to the time period over which the fixed asset is used.

In some circumstances we must take care to distinguish between capital and revenue expenditure. For example:

* *cost of building an extension to the factory £30,000, which includes £1,000 for repairs to the existing factory*

    – capital expenditure, £29,000

    – revenue expenditure, £1,000 (because it is for repairs to an existing fixed asset)

* *a plot of land has been bought for £20,000, the legal costs are £750*

    Capital expenditure £20,750 (the legal costs are included in the capital expenditure, because they are the cost of acquiring the fixed asset, ie the legal costs are capitalised).

- *own employees used to install a new air conditioning system: direct labour £1,000, materials £1,500*

  Capital expenditure £2,500 (an addition to the property). Note that, in cases such as this, revenue expenditure, ie direct labour and materials purchases, will need to be reduced to allow for the transfer to capital expenditure.

- *own employees used to repair and redecorate the premises: direct labour £500, materials £750*

  Revenue expenditure £1,250 (repairs and redecoration are running expenses).

- *purchase of a new machine £10,000, payment for installation and setting up £250*

  Capital expenditure £10,250 (costs of installation and setting up of a fixed asset are capitalised).

Only by allocating capital expenditure and revenue expenditure correctly can costs be ascertained properly and the profit and loss account and balance sheet reflect accurately the financial state of the business. It is especially important to identify revenue expenditure in the costing of output; a product that is costed wrongly (for example at too high a price) may not sell well because the selling price is too expensive for buyers. Identification of capital expenditure is important for knowing the assets owned by a business, which are shown on the balance sheet. If you, as an accounts assistant, are unsure about the allocation of costs between capital and revenue, you should always refer queries to the accounts supervisor.

DIRECT EXPENSES AND INDIRECT EXPENSES

For cost accounting purposes, revenue expenditure needs to be identified as either a direct expense or an indirect expense:

- direct expenses – those expenses which can be attributed to particular units of output
- indirect expenses – other expenses which cannot be attributed directly to particular units of output

The correct identification of these expenses will enable us to obtain a more accurate costing of each unit of output of the business or organisation.

direct expenses

Examples of direct expenses include:

- royalties payable to the designer of a product
- special items bought in for a particular product or job
- hire of specialist machinery/equipment for a particular product or job
- consultant's fees related to a particular product or job
- power costs of running machinery (provided that the machinery is separately metered and is used for a particular product or job)
- depreciation methods linked directly to output, eg units of output (or service) method

units of output depreciation

The units of output (or service) method of depreciation estimates:

- the number of units to be produced by a machine, or
- the number of hours of operation of a machine, or
- the number of miles/kilometres expected from a vehicle

over its expected life. Depreciation for a given year is calculated by reference to the number of units/hours/miles for that year.

For example, a machine costs £1,000. The total number of units of output to be produced by the machine over its life is expected to be 100,000. Therefore, each year's depreciation will be calculated at £100 for every 10,000 units produced (£1,000 ÷ 100,000 units). If year 1 production is 30,000 units, then depreciation of the machine will be £300 for the year. Over the machine's life of, say, four years, output and depreciation are as follows:

	output	depreciation
year 1	30,000 units	£300
year 2	25,000 units	£250
year 3	20,000 units	£200
year 4	25,000 units	£250
total	100,000 units	£1,000

indirect expenses

Examples of indirect expenses include:

- factory and office rent and rates
- telephone costs
- power costs of running machinery (where machinery is used for a variety of products or jobs, or where power consumption is low and it is not worthwhile for the costing system to analyse the amount of the direct expense)

- heating and lighting
- insurance
- cost of running motor vehicles
- depreciation methods not linked directly to output, eg straight-line and reducing balance methods

straight-line depreciation

A fixed percentage is written off the original cost of the asset each year, calculated by reference to the useful economic life of the asset as follows:

$$\frac{\text{cost of asset} - \text{estimated residual (scrap or salvage) sale proceeds}}{\text{number of years' expected use of the asset}}$$

For example, a machine costs £2,000, has an estimated life of four years, and an estimated scrap value at the end of four years of £400. The depreciation amount will be:

$$\frac{£2,000 - £400}{4 \text{ years}} = £400 \text{ per year (ie 20\% per year on cost)}$$

reducing balance depreciation

A fixed percentage is written off the reduced balance of the asset each year. The reduced balance is the cost of the asset less the provision for depreciation. For example, the machine seen earlier (which cost £2,000, has an estimated life of four years, and an estimated scrap value at the end of four years of £400) is to be depreciated by 33.3% (one-third) each year, using the reducing balance method. The depreciation amounts for the four years of ownership are:

	£
Original cost	2,000
Year 1 depreciation: 33.3% of £2,000	667
Value at end of year 1	1,333
Year 2 depreciation: 33.3% of £1,333	444
Value at end of year 2	889
Year 3 depreciation: 33.3% of £889	296
Value at end of year 3	593
Year 4 depreciation: 33.3% of £593	193
Value at end of year 4	400

Note: the figures have been rounded to the nearest £, and year 4 depreciation has been adjusted by £5 to leave a residual value of £400.

The formula to calculate the percentage of reducing balance depreciation is:

$$r = 1 - \sqrt[n]{\frac{s}{c}}$$

where:

r = percentage rate of depreciation

n = number of years

s = salvage (residual) value

c = cost of asset

In the example above the 33.3% is calculated as:

$$r = 1 - \sqrt[4]{\frac{400}{2,000}}$$

$$r = 1 - \sqrt[4]{0.2}$$ (to find the fourth root press the square root key on the calculator twice)

$$r = 1 - 0.669$$

$$r = 0.331 \text{ or } 33.1\% \text{ (which is close to the 33.3\% used above)}$$

BOOK-KEEPING FOR EXPENSES

The cost book-keeping entries to record expenses – the transfer of expenses to work-in-progress and to overheads – form part of the book-keeping system for costing.

The cost of direct expenses – which is attributable to output – is charged to work-in-progress. The cost of indirect expenses is charged to overheads and split between:

- production overheads
- non-production overheads, such as
  - selling and distribution
  - administration
  - finance

The cost book-keeping entries are:

- **transfer of direct expenses to work-in-progress**
  - debit work-in-progress account
  - credit expense account
- **transfer of indirect expenses to production overheads**
  - debit production overheads account
  - credit expense account
- **transfer of indirect expenses to non-production overheads**
  - debit non-production overheads account, eg selling and distribution, administration, finance
  - credit expense account

These cost book-keeping entries are shown diagrammatically as follows:

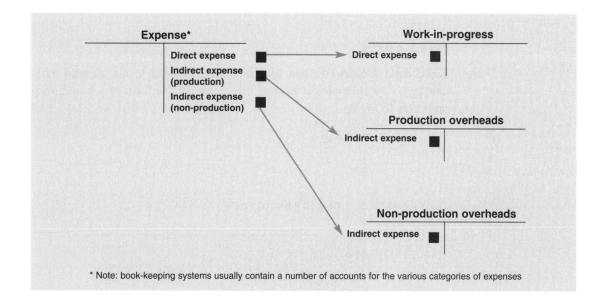

* Note: book-keeping systems usually contain a number of accounts for the various categories of expenses

Direct expenses are included with the costs of direct materials and direct labour to give a total of direct costs (prime cost). Indirect expenses are included in the total of indirect costs (overheads) of a business. For a service business, a major proportion of the costs are likely to be in the form of indirect costs; by contrast, a manufacturing business is likely to have a greater proportion of direct costs.

We shall be looking at the layout of the manufacturing account and the integrated book-keeping system for costing in Chapter 7.

FIXED AND VARIABLE COSTS

It is important in costing to appreciate the *nature of costs* – in particular to realise that not all costs increase or decrease in line with increases or decreases in output. As seen in Chapter 1 (page 21), 'Classification of costs by nature', all costs are:

- fixed, or
- semi-variable, or
- variable

We shall be studying the relationship between fixed and variable costs in detail later in the book (Chapter 8). In particular, we will be looking at the technique of break-even analysis – the point at which costs are exactly equal to income.

fixed costs

Fixed costs remain constant over a range of output levels, despite other changes – for example, insurance, rent, rates. In the form of a graph, they appear as follows:

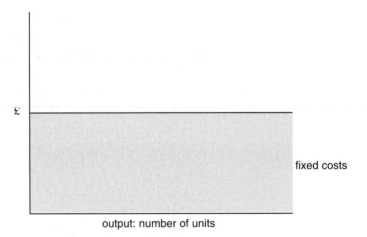

fixed costs

output: number of units

Note that money amounts are shown on the vertical axis and units of output on the horizontal axis.

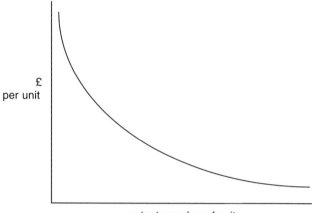

output: number of units

For fixed costs, the *cost per unit* falls as output increases, as follows:

For example, with rent of £40,000 per year:

- at output of 4,000 units, equals £10 per unit
- at output of 10,000 units, equals £4 per unit

Whilst it is sensible to seek to achieve maximum output in order to reduce the cost per unit, fixed costs do not remain fixed at all levels of production. For example, a decision to double production is likely to increase the fixed costs – an increase in factory rent, for example, because an additional factory may need to be rented. Fixed costs are often described as *stepped fixed costs,* because they increase by a large amount all at once; graphically, the cost behaviour is shown as a step:

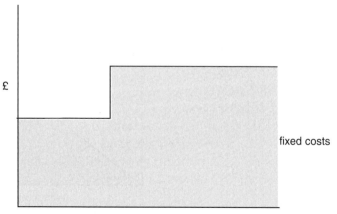

output: number of units

semi-variable costs

These combine both a fixed and a variable element. For example, a telephone bill comprises the fixed rental for the line, together with the variable element of call charges. Such a *mixed cost* is expressed graphically as:

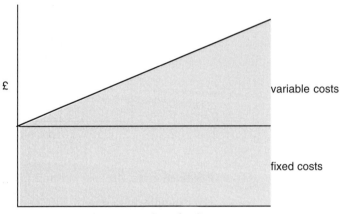

variable costs

Variable costs alter directly with changes in output levels, ie as activity increases, then the cost increases. Examples include direct materials, direct labour, direct expenses such as royalties. Graphically, variable costs appear as follows:

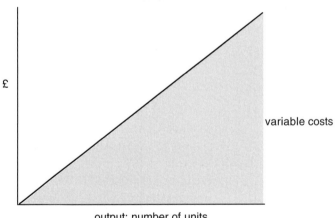

For example, a record company paying a royalty of £1 for each compact disc (CD) produced:

- at output of 1,000 CDs, equals variable cost of £1,000
- at output of 10,000 CDs, equals variable cost of £10,000

The cost per unit remains constant at all levels of output, as follows:

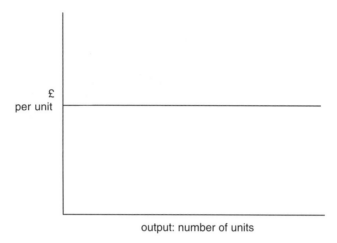

FIXED AND VARIABLE COSTS IN DECISION-MAKING

Identifying costs as being fixed, semi-variable or variable helps with decision-making – the business might be able to alter the balance between fixed and variable costs in order to increase profits. A product could be made:

- either, by using a labour-intensive process, with a large number of employees supported by basic machinery
- or, by using expensive machinery in an automated process with very few employees

In the first case, the cost structure will be high variable costs (direct labour) and low fixed costs (depreciation of machinery – assuming that straight-line or reducing balance depreciation methods are used). In the second case, there will be low variable costs, and high fixed costs. Management will need to examine the relationship between the costs – together with the likely sales figures, and the availability of finance with which to buy the machinery – before making a decision.

More specifically, a knowledge of the nature of costs can be used to help management to:

- identify the element of fixed costs within total costs
- prepare schedules of budgeted production costs
- identify the point at which costs are exactly equal to income – known as the break-even point (covered in Chapter 8)

IDENTIFYING THE ELEMENT OF FIXED COSTS

Where the total costs are known at two levels of output, the element of fixed costs can be identified using the 'high/low' technique.

example

- at output of 1,000 units, total costs are £7,000
- at output of 2,000 units, total costs are £9,000

What are the fixed costs?

Using the 'high/low' technique to identify the fixed costs:

- The high output and costs are deducted from the low output and costs, as follows:

	high output	2,000 units	£9,000
less	low output	1,000 units	£7,000
equals	difference	1,000 units	£2,000

- The amount of the variable cost per unit is now calculated as:

$$\frac{\text{change in cost}}{\text{change in units}} \quad = \quad \frac{£2,000}{1,000} \quad = \quad £2 \text{ variable cost per unit}$$

- Therefore, at 1,000 units of output the cost structure is:

	total cost	£7,000
less	variable costs (1,000 units x £2 per unit)	£2,000
equals	fixed costs	£5,000

- Check this now at 2,000 units of output when the cost structure is:

	variable costs (2,000 units x £2 per unit)	£4,000
add	fixed costs (as above)	£5,000
equals	total costs	£9,000

Note that the 'high/low' technique can only be used when variable costs increase by the same money amount for each extra unit of output (ie there is a linear relationship), and where there are no stepped fixed costs.

SCHEDULES OF BUDGETED PRODUCTION COSTS

Where fixed and variable costs are known for the three elements of costs – materials, labour and expenses – at a particular level of output, it is relatively simple to calculate what the costs will be at changed levels of output. For example, if variable materials costs at an output of 1,000 units are £2,000 then, at an output of 1,100 units, they will be £2,200 (ie a 10 per cent increase in both output and cost). By contrast, the fixed expense of factory rent of, say, £5,000 will be unchanged if output increases by 10 per cent. (Note that such calculations assume a linear relationship for variable costs and that there are no stepped fixed costs.)

Such changes in costs can be incorporated, as part of a business' planning process, into a formal schedule of *budgeted production costs.* This calculates total production cost and the cost per unit at changed (either increased or decreased) levels of output, as shown in the Case Study which follows.

Case Study

SPEEDPEN LTD: BUDGETED PRODUCTION COSTS

situation

Speedpen Limited, which manufactures quality rollerball pens, has budgeted its production costs for 2008 on the basis of an output of 100,000 units as follows:

			£
•	variable costs	– materials	75,000
		– labour	50,000
		– expenses	10,000
•	fixed costs	– labour	22,500
		– overheads	33,500

The sales department thinks that demand for the product is more likely to be 110,000 units, or could be as high as 125,000 units.

You have been asked to prepare a budgeted cost schedule based on outputs of 100,000 units, 110,000 units and 125,000 units. The cost schedule is to show total production cost and the cost per unit at each level of output.

solution

2008	**BUDGETED PRODUCTION COSTS**		
UNITS	100,000	110,000	125,000
COSTS	£	£	£
Variable costs			
Materials	75,000	82,500	93,750
Labour	50,000	55,000	62,500
Expenses	10,000	11,000	12,500
	135,000	148,500	168,750
Fixed costs			
Labour	22,500	22,500	22,500
Overheads	33,500	33,500	33,500
	56,000	56,000	56,000
TOTAL PRODUCTION COST	191,000	204,500	224,750
COST PER UNIT	£1.91	£1.86	£1.80

Notes:

- Variable costs per unit are: materials, £0.75 (ie £75,000 ÷ 100,000 units); labour, £0.50; expenses, £0.10
- At the higher levels of output simply multiply the unit costs by 110,000 and 125,000
- Fixed costs remain fixed at the higher levels of output
- Total production cost is total variable costs plus total fixed costs
- Cost per unit is total production cost divided by output (note that cost per unit has been rounded to the nearest penny)
- The costs at higher levels of output assume that:
  - there is a linear relationship for variable costs
  - there are no stepped fixed costs
- The fall in cost per unit as output increases occurs because the fixed costs are being spread over a greater number of units, ie the fixed cost per unit falls

Chapter Summary

- Expenses, together with materials and labour, form the three main elements of cost.

- Expenses are categorised between:
  - capital expenditure and revenue expenditure
  - direct expenses and indirect expenses
  - fixed costs and variable costs

- Identification of revenue expenditure is important in the costing of output; identification of capital expenditure is important for knowing the assets owned by a business.

- Direct expenses are charged to work-in-progress.

- Indirect expenses are charged to overheads and split between:
  - production overheads
  - non-production overheads, such as selling and distribution, administration, finance

- The nature of costs means that not all costs increase or decrease in line with increases or decreases in output; all costs, by nature, are:
  - fixed, or
  - semi-variable, or
  - variable

- A knowledge of the nature of costs enables:
  - identification of the element of fixed costs within total costs
  - preparation of a schedule of budgeted production costs
  - identification of the break-even point

Key Terms

capital expenditure	expenditure incurred on the purchase, alteration or improvement of fixed assets
revenue expenditure	expenditure incurred on running costs
direct expenses	those expenses that are attributable to particular units of output
indirect expenses	all other expenses which are not attributable directly to particular units of output

overheads	the indirect costs of materials, labour and expenses
fixed costs	costs which remain fixed over a range of output levels
semi-variable costs	costs which combine a fixed and variable element
variable costs	costs which vary directly with output
'high/low' technique	method used to identify the element of fixed costs within total costs
budgeted production costs	schedule which shows the calculation of total production cost and cost per unit at particular levels of output

Student Activities

4.1 Define:

(a)   capital expenditure

(b)   revenue expenditure

Give two examples of each.

4.2 Define:

(a)   direct expenses

(b)   indirect expenses

Give two examples of each.

4.3 Fred Jarvis normally works as a production-line employee of Wyevale Plastics. However, for the past four weeks he has been building an extension to the company's warehouse.

How should his wages for this period be dealt with in the accounts? Why is this?

4.4 Explain the nature of the costs, as shown by the following graphs:

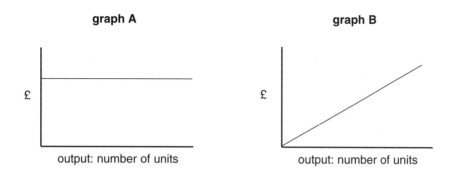

Graph (a) shows the cost of the rent of a factory.

Graph (b) shows the wages of production-line employees who are paid on a piecework basis.

4.5 Classify the following costs (tick the appropriate column):

	capital expenditure	revenue expenditure
(a) purchase of motor vehicles		
(b) depreciation of motor vehicles		
(c) payment of office rent		
(d) salaries of office staff		
(e) legal fees relating to the purchase of property		
(f) re-decoration of office		
(g) installation of air-conditioning in office		
(h) wages of own employees used to build extension to the stockroom		
(i) installation and setting up of a new machine		

4.6 Classify the following costs (tick the appropriate column):

		direct expenses	indirect expenses	either*
(a)	hire of machinery for a particular job			
(b)	office rent			
(c)	cleaning materials			
(d)	power costs			
(e)	royalty paid to designer for each unit of output			
(f)	sales staff car expenses			
(g)	depreciation of production machinery			
(h)	consultant's fees relating to a particular job			
(i)	heating and lighting			

*explain your reasons for classifying costs in this column

4.11 Monica Manufacturing has budgeted the production costs for 2008 on the basis of an output of 250,000 units as follows:

		£
variable costs	– materials	400,000
	– labour	325,000
	– expenses	100,000
fixed costs	– labour	96,500
	– overheads	107,500

The sales department thinks that demand for the product is more likely to be 300,000 units, or could be as high as 350,000 units.

You are to prepare a schedule of budgeted production costs based on outputs of 250,000 units, 300,000 units and 350,000 units. The schedule is to show total production cost and the cost per unit at each level of output. (Note: you may assume that there is a linear relationship for variable costs, and that there are no stepped fixed costs.)

Briefly describe and explain the trend in costs per unit for the three budgeted levels of production.

5 Overheads

this chapter covers . . .

- the need to recover the cost of overheads through units of output
- the process of allocating and apportioning the cost of overheads into the units of output
- the different bases of apportionment of overheads
- apportionment of service department costs
- the commonly-used overhead absorption rates and their relative merits in given circumstances
- the book-keeping entries for overheads

PERFORMANCE CRITERIA COVERED

unit 6: RECORDING AND ANALYSING COSTS AND REVENUES

element 6.2

record and analyse information relating to the allocation, apportionment and absorption of overhead costs

A   identify overhead costs in accordance with the organisation's procedures

B   attribute overhead costs to production and service cost centres in accordance with agreed bases of allocation and apportionment

C   calculate overhead absorption rates in accordance with the agreed bases of absorption

D   record and analyse information relating to overhead costs in accordance with the organisation's procedures

E   make adjustments for under and over recovered overhead costs in accordance with established procedures

F   review methods of allocation, apportionment and absorption at regular intervals in discussions with senior staff and ensure agreed changes to methods are implemented

G   consult staff working in operational departments to resolve any queries in overhead cost data

OVERHEADS

In Chapter 1 'An Introduction to Cost Accounting' we saw that costs could be classified as follows:

DIRECT MATERIALS	INDIRECT MATERIALS
+ DIRECT LABOUR	+ INDIRECT LABOUR
+ DIRECT EXPENSES	+ INDIRECT EXPENSES
= TOTAL DIRECT COSTS (PRIME COST)	= TOTAL OVERHEADS

Direct costs can be identified directly with each unit of output, but indirect costs (overheads) cannot be identified directly with each unit of output.

Overheads do not relate to particular units of output but must, instead, be shared amongst all the cost units (units of output to which costs can be charged) to which they relate. For example, the cost of the factory rent must be included in the cost of the firm's output.

The important point to remember is that all the overheads of a business, together with the direct costs (materials, labour and expenses) must be covered by money flowing in from the firm's output – the sales of products or services. This point is demonstrated in the Case Study which follows.

Case Study

COOLHEADS: A HAIRDRESSING BUSINESS

situation

CoolHeads is a new hairdressing business, being set up by Nathan and Morgan in a rented shop.

Nathan and Morgan are preparing their price list. They must set the prices sufficiently high to cover all their costs and to give them a profit.

They have details of the costs of all the materials they need (shampoos, colourings and so on) from a specialist supplier. Nathan and Morgan have decided the rate to charge to the business for their own work and they do not intend to employ anyone else for the time being.

But there are other costs which they will also incur – their overheads – and they are not so sure how they will work these into their pricing structure. Nathan asks:

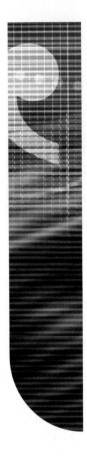

'What about the shop rent and the business rates we have to pay? What about the electricity, the insurance, the telephone bill and all the advertising we have to do? How are we going to cover these costs?'

'How much will it cost us in total to deal with each customer?'

'How do we make sure that we are going to make a profit?'

solution

For pricing purposes, Nathan and Morgan need to include overheads in the cost of each item on their price list.

In a small business like this, the whole business could be a single cost centre. All the overheads could be allowed for in a single rate to charge for a hair cut.

Suppose Nathan and Morgan estimate that their total overheads for the first year of trading will be £27,000. They expect to be working on hairstyling for 1,500 hours each during the year, ie a total of 3,000 hours between them.

Therefore, they could decide in advance that each hour of their work should be charged £27,000 ÷ 3,000 = £9 for overheads. A job that takes two hours to complete would then be charged 2 x £9 = £18 for overheads.

Notice that in a service business such as hairdressing, direct materials costs are likely to be relatively small in comparison with the cost of direct labour and overheads. It is essential for Nathan and Morgan to consider the cost of overheads when they are setting their prices and the hourly rate is one possible way of doing this. This is called an 'overhead absorption rate' and we will look in more detail at this idea later in this chapter (page 128).

In larger businesses and organisations, overheads are usually classified by function under headings such as:

- factory or production, eg factory rent and rates, indirect factory labour, indirect factory materials, heating and lighting of factory
- selling and distribution, eg salaries of sales staff, vehicle costs, delivery costs
- administration, eg office rent and rates, office salaries, heating and lighting of office, indirect office materials
- finance, eg bank interest

Each of these functions or sections of the business is likely to be what is known as a cost centre, a term which was defined in Chapter 1 as follows:

Cost centres are sections of a business to which costs can be charged.

In order to deal with the overheads we need to know how the whole organisation is split into cost centres. This will depend on the size of the business and the way in which the work is organised.

COLLECTING OVERHEADS IN COST CENTRES

allocation of overheads

Some overheads belong entirely to one particular cost centre, for example:

- the salary of a supervisor who works in only one cost centre

- the rent of a separate building in which there is only one cost centre

- the cost of indirect materials that have been issued to one particular cost centre

Overheads like these can therefore be allocated to the cost centre to which they belong.

Allocation of overheads is the charging to a particular cost centre of overheads that are incurred entirely by that cost centre.

apportionment of overheads

Overheads that cannot be allocated to a particular cost centre have to be shared or **apportioned** between two or more cost centres.

Apportionment of overheads is the sharing of overheads over a number of cost centres to which they relate. Each cost centre is charged with a proportion of the overhead cost.

For example, a department which is a cost centre within a factory will be charged a proportion of the factory rent and rates. Another example is where a supervisor works within two departments, both of which are separate cost centres: the indirect labour cost of employing the supervisor is shared between the two cost centres.

With apportionment, a suitable **basis** – or method – must be found to apportion overheads between cost centres; the basis selected should be related to the type of cost. Different methods might be used for each overhead.

Look at the example on the next page.

OVERHEAD	BASIS OF APPORTIONMENT
rent, rates	floor area (or volume of space) of cost centres
heating, lighting	floor area (or volume of space) of cost centres
buildings insurance	floor area (or volume of space) of cost centres
buildings depreciation	floor area (or volume of space) of cost centres
machinery insurance	cost or net book value of machinery and equipment
machinery depreciation	value of machinery; or machine usage (hours)
canteen	number of employees in each cost centre
supervisory costs	number of employees in each cost centre, or labour hours worked by supervisors in each cost centre

It must be stressed that apportionment is used for those overheads that cannot be allocated to a particular cost centre. For example, if a college's Business Studies Department occupies a building in another part of town from the main college building, the rates for the building can clearly be allocated to the Business Studies cost centre. By contrast, the rates for the main college building must be apportioned amongst the cost centres on the main campus.

review of allocation and apportionment

It is important that the allocation and apportionment of overheads are reviewed at regular intervals to ensure that the methods being used are still valid. For example:

- *allocation*

  The role of a supervisor may have changed – whereas previously the supervisor worked in one department only, he or she might now be working in two departments

- *apportionment*

  Building work may have expanded the floor area of a department, so that the apportionment basis needs to be reworked

Any proposed changes to allocation and apportionment must be discussed with senior staff and their agreement obtained before any changes to methods are implemented. Accounting staff will often have to consult with staff (such as managers and supervisors) working in operational departments, to discuss how overheads are charged to their departments, and to resolve any queries.

apportionment and ratios

It is important to understand the method of apportionment of overheads using ratios. For example, overheads relating to buildings are often shared in the ratio of the floor area used by the cost centres.

Now read through the Worked Example and the Case Study which follow.

WORKED EXAMPLE: APPORTIONMENT USING RATIOS

A business has four cost centres: two production departments, A and B, and two non-production cost centres, stores and maintenance. The total rent per year for the business premises is £12,000. This is to be apportioned on the basis of floor area, given as:

	production dept A	production dept B	stores	maintenance
Floor area (square metres)	400	550	350	200

Step 1
Calculate the total floor area: 400 + 550 + 350 + 200 = 1,500 square metres

Step 2
Divide the total rent by the total floor area: £12,000 ÷ 1,500 = £8
This gives a rate of £8 per square metre.

Step 3
Multiply the floor area in each cost centre by the rate per square metre. This gives the share of rent for each cost centre. For example, in Production Department A, the share of rent is 400 x £8 = £3,200. The results are shown in the table:

	production dept A	production dept B	stores	maintenance
Floor area (square metres)	400	550	350	200
Rent apportioned	£3,200	£4,400	£2,800	£1,600

Step 4
Check that the apportioned amounts agree with the total rent:
£3,200 + £4,400 + £ 2,800 + £1,600 = £12,000.

PILOT ENGINEERING LIMITED:
OVERHEAD ALLOCATION AND APPORTIONMENT

situation

Pilot Engineering Limited, which makes car engine components, uses some of the latest laser equipment in one department, while another section of the business continues to use traditional machinery. Details of the factory are as follows:

Department X is a 'hi-tech' machine shop equipped with laser-controlled machinery which cost £80,000. This department has 400 square metres of floor area. There are three machine operators: the supervisor spends one-third of the time in this department.

Department Y is a 'low-tech' part of the factory equipped with machinery which cost £20,000. The floor area is 600 square metres. There are two workers who spend all their time in this department: the supervisor spends two-thirds of the time in this department.

The overheads to be allocated or apportioned are as follows:

1	Factory rates	£12,000
2	Wages of the supervisor	£21,000
3	Factory heating and lighting	£2,500
4	Depreciation of machinery	£20,000
5	Buildings insurance	£2,000
6	Insurance of machinery	£1,500
7	Specialist materials for the laser equipment	£2,500

How should each of these be allocated or apportioned to each department?

solution

The recommendations are:

1 Factory rates – apportioned on the basis of floor area.

2 Supervisor's wages – apportioned on the basis of time spent, ie one-third to Department X, and two-thirds to Department Y. If the time spent was not known, an alternative basis could be established, based on the number of employees.

3 Factory heating and lighting – apportioned on the basis of floor area.

4 Depreciation of machinery – apportioned on the basis of machine value.

5 Buildings insurance – apportioned on the basis of floor area.

6 Insurance of machinery – apportioned on the basis of machine value.

7 Specialist materials for the laser equipment – allocated to Department X because this cost belongs entirely to Department X.

It is important to note that there are no fixed rules for the apportionment of overheads – the only proviso is that a fair proportion of the overhead is charged to each department which has some responsibility for the cost being incurred. Methods of apportionment will need to be reviewed at regular intervals to ensure that they are still valid; changes can only be implemented with the agreement of senior staff.

The apportionment of overheads for Pilot Engineering Limited is as follows (sample workings are shown below the table):

overhead	basis of apportionment	total	dept X	dept Y
		£	£	£
Factory rates	Floor area	12,000	4,800	7,200
Wages of supervisor	Time spent	21,000	7,000	14,000
Heating and lighting	Floor area	2,500	1,000	1,500
Dep'n of machinery	Machine value	20,000	16,000	4,000
Buildings insurance	Floor area	2,000	800	1,200
Machinery insurance	Machine value	1,500	1,200	300
Specialist materials	Allocation	2,500	2,500	–
		61,500	33,300	28,200

workings

For example, the floor areas of the two departments are:

Dept X	400	square metres
Dept Y	600	square metres
Total	1,000	square metres

Factory rates are apportioned as follows:

$$\frac{£12,000}{1,000} = £12 \text{ per square metre}$$

Dept X rates:	£12 x 400 =	£4,800
Dept Y rates	£12 x 600 =	£7,200
Total (check)		£12,000

Note that overhead apportionment is often, in practice, calculated using a computer spreadsheet.

SERVICE DEPARTMENTS

Many businesses have departments which provide services within the business; for example, maintenance, transport, stores or stationery. Each service department is likely to be a cost centre, to which a proportion of overheads is charged. As service departments do not themselves have any cost units to which their overheads may be charged, the costs of each service department must be re-apportioned to the production departments (which do have cost units to which overheads can be charged). A suitable basis of re-allocation must be used, for example:

- the overheads of a maintenance department might be re-apportioned to production departments on the basis of value of machinery or equipment, or on the basis of time spent in each production department
- the overheads of a stores or stationery department could be re-apportioned on the basis of value of goods issued to production departments
- the overheads of a subsidised canteen could be re-apportioned on the basis of the number of employees

Re-apportionment of service department overheads is considered in the next section.

RE-APPORTIONMENT OF SERVICE DEPARTMENT OVERHEADS

The overheads of service departments are charged to production cost centres using one of the following techniques:

- **direct apportionment** is used where service departments provide services to production departments only
- the **step-down method** is used where service departments provide services to production departments and to some other service departments

To illustrate re-apportionment, we will apply these techniques to a business with two production departments, A and B, and two service departments, stores and maintenance. After allocation and apportionment of production overheads, the totals are:

	total	production dept A	production dept B	stores	maintenance
	£	£	£	£	£
Overheads	20,400	10,000	5,000	2,400	3,000

direct apportionment

Here the service departments do not provide services to one another. Their costs are directly apportioned to production departments using a suitable basis. In the example on the previous page:

- stores overheads are re-apportioned on the basis of the number of stores requisitions – department A has made 150 requisitions; department B has made 50

- maintenance overheads are re-apportioned on the value of machinery – department A has machinery with a net book value of £20,000, department B's machinery has a value of £10,000

Using direct apportionment, the overheads of the service departments are re-apportioned as shown in the table below. The method of calculation using ratios is the same as we used for apportionment.

Notice that the total is taken out of the service cost centre column when it is shared between the production cost centres.

	total	production dept A	production dept B	stores	maintenance
	£	£	£	£	£
Overheads	20,400	10,000	5,000	2,400	3,000
Stores	–	1,800	600	(2,400)	–
Maintenance	–	2,000	1,000	–	(3,000)
	20,400	13,800	6,600	–	–

Thus all the overheads have now been charged to the production departments where they can be 'absorbed' into the cost units which form the output of each department. We will see how the absorption is carried out later in this chapter.

step-down method

This is used where, as well as to production departments, one service department provides services to another. Using the example, the stores department deals with requisitions from the maintenance department, but no maintenance work is carried out in the stores department. Under the step-down method we re-apportion firstly the overheads of the stores department (because it does not receive any services from the maintenance department), and secondly the overheads of the maintenance department:

- stores requisitions
  - department A   150
  - department B   50
  - maintenance   50
- value of machinery
  - department A   £20,000
  - department B   £10,000

The re-apportionment of the production overheads of the service departments, using the step-down method, is as follows:

	total	production dept A	production dept B	stores	maintenance
	£	£	£	£	£
Overheads	20,400	10,000	5,000	2,400	3,000
Stores	–	1,440	480	(2,400)	480
				–	*3,480
Maintenance	–	2,320	1,160	–	(3,480)
	20,400	13,760	6,640	–	–

* Note that a new total is calculated for the maintenance department before it is re-apportioned. £480 from stores is added to the original £3,000 overheads in the maintenance department.

All the overheads have now been charged to the production departments.

ALLOCATION AND APPORTIONMENT – A SUMMARY

The diagram on the next page summarises the allocation and apportionment of overheads that we have seen in this chapter. It shows:

- allocation of overheads directly to cost centres
- apportionment of overheads on an equitable basis to cost centres
- re-apportionment of service department costs to production cost centres

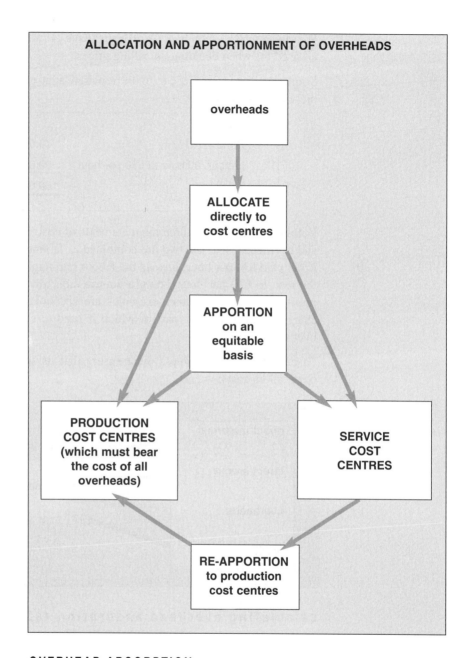

ALLOCATION AND APPORTIONMENT OF OVERHEADS

overheads

ALLOCATE
directly to
cost centres

APPORTION
on an
equitable
basis

PRODUCTION
COST CENTRES
(which must bear
the cost of all
overheads)

SERVICE
COST
CENTRES

RE-APPORTION
to production
cost centres

OVERHEAD ABSORPTION

Once overheads have been allocated or apportioned to production cost
centres, the final step is to ensure that the overheads are charged to cost
units. In the language of cost accounting this is known as 'absorption' or
'recovery', ie the cost of overheads is charged to the cost units which pass
through that particular production department.

We saw in the Case Study of CoolHeads (page 117), how overheads could be allowed for when deciding on selling prices.

Similarly, if you take a car to be repaired at a garage, the bill may be presented as follows:

	£
Parts	70.00
Labour: 3 hours at £30 per hour	90.00
Total	160.00

Within this bill are the three main elements of cost: materials (parts), labour and overheads. The last two are combined as labour – the garage mechanic is not paid £30 per hour; instead the labour rate might be £10 per hour, with the rest, ie £20 per hour, being a contribution towards the overheads and profit of the garage. Other examples are accountants and solicitors, who charge a 'rate per hour', part of which is used to contribute to the cost of overheads and profit.

To be profitable, a business must ensure that its selling prices more than cover all its costs:

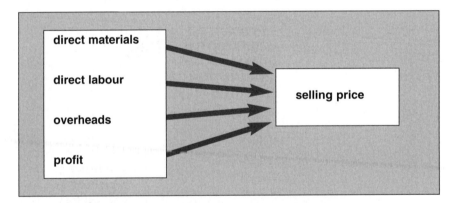

calculating overhead absorption rates

In order to absorb the overheads of a department, there are two steps to be followed:

1 calculation of the overhead absorption rate (OAR)

2 application of this rate to actual work done

The overhead absorption rate is calculated using estimated or budgeted figures as follows, for a given time period:

$$OAR = \frac{\textit{total budgeted cost centre overheads}}{\textit{total planned work in the cost centre}}$$

The amount of work must be measured in a suitable way, usually:

- direct labour hours, or

- machine hours

These methods are illustrated below.

direct labour hour method of calculation

With this method, production overhead is absorbed on the basis of the number of direct labour hours worked.

1 Calculation of the overhead absorption rate, using budgeted (expected) figures:

$$\frac{\textit{total cost centre overheads}}{\textit{total direct labour hours (in cost centre)}} = \textit{cost per direct labour hour}$$

2 Application of the rate:

direct labour hours worked x overhead absorption rate

= overhead absorbed

Example

Department A   total budgeted cost centre overheads for year   £40,000

     expected direct labour hours for year   5,000

     actual direct labour hours in March   450

1   Overhead absorption rate:

$$\frac{£40,000}{5,000 \text{ hours}} = £8 \text{ per direct labour hour}$$

2   Application of the rate:

450 hours x £8 = £3,600 of overhead absorbed in March

machine hour method of calculation

Here the production overhead is absorbed on the basis of machine hours.

1 Calculation of the overhead absorption rate, using budgeted (expected) figures:

$$\frac{\textit{total cost centre overheads}}{\textit{total machine hours (in cost centre)}} = \textit{cost per machine hour}$$

2   Application of the rate:

machine hours worked x overhead absorption rate

= overhead absorbed

Example

Department B   total budgeted cost centre overheads for year   £216,000
                      expected machine hours for year   36,000
                      actual machine hours in March   3,500

1   Overhead absorption rate:

$$\frac{£216,000}{36,000 \text{ hours}} \quad = \quad £6 \text{ per machine hour}$$

2   Application of the rate:
         3,500 hours x £6 = £21,000 of overhead absorbed in March

which method to use?

Only one overhead absorption rate will be used in a particular department, and the method selected must relate to the reason why the costs are incurred. For example, a cost centre which is machine based, where most of the overheads incurred relate to machinery, will use a machine hour basis.

The direct labour hour method is a very popular method (eg the garage mentioned earlier) because overheads are absorbed on a time basis. Thus the cost unit that requires twice the direct labour of another cost unit will be charged twice the overhead. However this method will be inappropriate where some units are worked on by hand while others quickly pass through a machinery process and require little direct labour time.

A machine hour rate is particularly appropriate where expensive machinery is used in the department. However, it would be unsuitable where not all products pass through the machine but some are worked on by hand: in the latter case, no overheads would be charged to the cost units.

It is important to select the best method of overhead absorption for the particular business, otherwise wrong decisions will be made on the basis of the costing information. The particular absorption method selected for a department will need to be reviewed at regular intervals to ensure that it is still valid. For example, the direct labour hour method is unlikely to continue to be appropriate where a machine has been brought in to automate processes that were previously carried out by hand. Any proposed changes must be discussed with senior staff and their agreement obtained before any changes to methods are implemented. The changes will need to be discussed with staff (such as managers and supervisors) working in operational departments to explain how overheads will be charged to their departments in the future, and any queries will need to be resolved.

In this chapter, we have calculated overhead absorption rates based on:

* direct labour hours

* machine hours

There are other possible bases which could be used. For example, overheads could be charged as a percentage of:

* direct material cost

* direct labour cost

* prime cost

The principles are the same for any method of absorption:

* the rate to use is calculated in advance using estimates

* the rate is applied to the actual work done

For example, if the estimates showed that it would be necessary to add 20% on to prime cost for overheads, then a job having a prime cost of £6,000 would absorb £6,000 x 20% = £1,200 of overheads, making a total of £7,200.

using a pre-determined rate

Most businesses and organisations calculate a pre-determined overhead absorption rate for each department. This is then applied to all production passing through that department.

The OAR is calculated in advance using estimates – this avoids having to calculate the rate regularly, which may result in changes over quite short time periods. Instead the rate is smoothed out over fluctuations in cost and activity over a longer accounting period.

OVER- OR UNDER-ABSORPTION OF OVERHEADS

In the Case Study of CoolHeads (page 117) we saw that Nathan and Morgan estimated that their total overheads for the first year of trading would be £27,000. They expected to be working on hairstyling for 1,500 hours each during the year, ie a total of 3,000 hours between them.

Therefore, they could have decided in advance that each hour of their work should be charged £27,000/3,000 = £9 for overheads. A job taking two hours to complete would then be charged 2 x £9 = £18 for overheads. This is a simple example of the absorption of overheads using a pre-determined rate. (The word 'recovery' is sometimes used instead of 'absorption' – it means the same.)

At the end of CoolHeads' first year, it is most unlikely that Nathan and Morgan will find that everything went exactly according to plan. They may have spent more or less on the overheads than £27,000. They may have worked on styling for more or less than 3,000 hours in total.

They will find, therefore, that the amount of overheads they have absorbed into the cost of their actual work during the year is not the same as the amount they have spent. If the amount absorbed is the greater, the difference is called 'over-absorption' or 'over-recovery' of overheads. If the amount absorbed is less than the amount spent, the difference is called 'under-absorption' or 'under-recovery'.

Over-absorption or under-absorption (recovery) is the difference between the total amount of overheads absorbed (recovered) in a given period and the total amount spent on overheads.

The following worked example shows the calculation when the overhead absorption rate is based on direct labour hours.

Example

Department C

overhead absorption rate (based on direct labour hours)	£6.00 per labour hour
actual labour hours in year	6,300 hours
actual overheads for year	£36,000

- actual overheads for the department are £36,000
- actual overhead absorbed: 6,300 hours x £6.00 per hour = £37,800
- over-absorption of overhead: £37,800 – £36,000 = £1,800

At the end of the financial year, an adjustment is made to profit and loss account for the total over-absorbed or under-absorbed overhead.

On first impressions, over-absorption of overheads seems to be a 'bonus' for a business – profits will be higher; however, it should be remembered that the overhead rate may have been set too high. As a consequence, sales might have been lost because the selling price has been too high. The OAR will need to be reviewed if over-absorption continues on a regular basis.

In the next section we see the book-keeping entries to record the over-absorption or under-absorption of overheads.

BOOK-KEEPING ENTRIES FOR OVERHEADS

In this section we look at the cost book-keeping entries to record the transfer of the cost of overheads to work-in-progress, together with the entries for over- or under-absorption of overheads (which are transferred to profit and loss account). These entries form part of the book-keeping system for costing; Chapter 7 looks in detail at an integrated book-keeping system.

A production overheads account is used to:

- transfer production overheads to work-in-progress
- credit the amount of over-absorbed overheads to profit and loss account
- charge the amount of under-absorbed overheads to profit and loss account

The cost book-keeping entries are:

- **transfer production overheads to work-in-progress**
  - – debit work-in-progress account
  - – credit production overheads account

- **credit over-absorbed overheads to profit and loss account**
  - – debit production overheads account
  - – credit profit and loss account

  Here, the amount of over-absorbed overheads reduces the total cost of production, and so increases profits.

- **charge under-absorbed overheads to profit and loss account**
  - – debit profit and loss account
  - – credit production overheads account

  Here the amount of under-absorbed overheads adds to the total cost of production, and so reduces profits.

These cost book-keeping entries are shown diagrammatically as shown on the next page.

The cost book-keeping entries are:

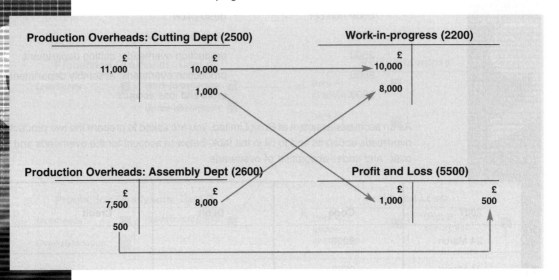

Production Overheads: Cutting Dept (2500)		Work-in-progress (2200)
£ 11,000	£ 10,000	£ 10,000
	1,000	8,000

Production Overheads: Assembly Dept (2600)		Profit and Loss (5500)
£ 7,500	£ 8,000	£ 1,000	£ 500
500		

The cost book-keeping entries are recorded on the table as follows:

2007	Code	Debit	Credit
24 March	2200	£10,000	
24 March	2500		£10,000
24 March	2200	£8,000	
24 March	2600		£8,000
24 March	5500	£1,000	
24 March	2500		£1,000
24 March	2600	£500	
24 March	5500		£500

In this way, the cost of the pre-determined overhead rates is charged to work-in-progress, while the amount of over- or under-absorption of overheads is transferred to profit and loss account.

- Direct costs can be charged directly to cost units.

- Indirect costs (overheads) cannot be charged to cost units immediately.

- Overheads are:
  - allocated to a specific cost centre, if they belong entirely to that cost centre
  - apportioned between cost centres, if they are shared

- Apportionment is done on a suitable basis, using ratios of floor area, numbers of employees and so on.

- Methods of allocation and apportionment should be reviewed regularly.

- The total overheads allocated and apportioned to the service cost centres are then re-apportioned to the production cost centres.

- After re-apportionment of the service cost centre overheads, the total overheads in each production cost centre can be calculated.

- All the above steps can be carried out using expected or budgeted overhead amounts.

- Overhead absorption rates are calculated using the total expected or budgeted overheads in each cost centre.

- An overhead absorption rate is calculated as follows:

  $$overhead\ absorption\ rate\ =\ \frac{total\ budgeted\ cost\ centre\ overheads}{total\ planned\ work\ in\ cost\ centre}$$

  where the planned amount of work may be measured, often in terms of direct labour hours or machine hours.

- Overhead absorption rates are applied to the actual work carried out. A direct labour hour absorption rate is applied as follows, for example:

  Direct labour hours worked x overhead absorption rate

  = overhead absorbed

- At the end of a given period, the amount of overhead absorbed may differ from the amount actually spent on the overheads. The difference is either an over-absorption (when the amount absorbed is greater than the amount spent) or an under-absorption (when the amount absorbed is less than the amount spent).

- Cost book-keeping entries are made to record:
  - the transfer of overheads to work-in-progress
  - the transfer of over- or under-absorption of overheads to profit and loss account

overheads	indirect costs, made up of
	indirect materials + indirect labour + indirect expenses
cost centres	sections of a business to which costs can be charged
allocation of overheads	the charging to a particular cost centre of overheads that are incurred entirely by that cost centre
apportionment of overheads	the sharing of overheads over a number of cost centres to which they relate – each cost centre is charged with a proportion of the overhead cost
service department	a non-production cost centre that provides services to other cost centres in the business
re-apportionment of service department overheads	the sharing of the total overheads from a service department, a proportion being charged to each cost centre it serves; after all re-apportionment has been carried out, the overheads will be charged to production cost centres only
absorption (recovery) of overheads	the charging of overheads to cost units (units of output)
overhead absorption rate (OAR)	the rate used to charge overheads to cost units – calculated in advance, as:
	budgeted total overhead ÷ planned amount of work
basis of absorption	the measurement of work used to calculate the overhead absorption rate, for example:
	• direct labour hours
	• machine hours
over- or under-absorption (recovery)	the difference between the total amount of overheads absorbed (recovered) in a given period and the total amount spent on overheads

Student Activities

5.1 Distinguish between:
- allocation of overheads
- apportionment of overheads

5.2 Wyvern Fabrication Company has two production departments – moulding and finishing.

The company charges overheads on the basis of machine hours and the following overhead analysis information is available to you (note that service department overheads have already been apportioned to production departments):

OVERHEAD ANALYSIS SHEET		
	MOULDING	FINISHING
Budgeted total overheads (£)	9,338	3,298
Budgeted machine hours	1,450	680
Budgeted overhead absorption rate (£)		

Details of a particular job of work are as follows:

JOB OVERHEAD ANALYSIS SHEET		
	MOULDING	FINISHING
Job machine hours	412	154
Budgeted overhead absorption rate (£)		
Overhead absorbed by job (£)		

You are to:

(a) Calculate the overhead absorption rate for each of the two departments and complete the overhead analysis sheet.

(b) Calculate the production overhead absorbed by the job and complete the job overhead analysis sheet.

(c) Suggest two other overhead absorption rates that the company might use and comment on the circumstances that would make them appropriate.

5.3 ABC Limited is a manufacturing business with three cost centres: Departments A, B and C. The following are the expected factory overheads for the forthcoming year:

Rent and rates	£7,210
Depreciation of machinery	£10,800
Supervisor's salary	£12,750
Insurance of machinery	£750

Departmental information is:

	Dept A	Dept B	Dept C
Floor area (sq m)	300	150	250
Value of machinery	£25,000	£15,000	£10,000
Number of production-line employees	8	4	3

You are to:

(a) Apportion the overheads to the cost centres, stating the basis of apportionment.

(b) Calculate the overhead absorption rate (to two decimal places) of each department, based on direct labour hours. Note that the factory works a 37 hour week for 48 weeks in a year.

5.4 Wye Engineering Limited offers specialist engineering services to the car industry. It has two production departments – machining and finishing – and a service department which maintains the machinery of both departments. Expected production overheads for the forthcoming year are:

	£
Rent and rates	5,520
Buildings insurance	1,320
Insurance of machinery	1,650
Lighting and heating	3,720
Depreciation of machinery	11,000
Supervisory salaries	30,000
Maintenance department salary	16,000
Factory cleaning	4,800

The following information is available:

	Machining	Finishing	Maintenance
Floor area (square metres)	300	200	100
Number of employees	6	3	1
Value of machinery	£40,000	£15,000	–

The factory works a 35 hour week for 47 weeks each year.

You are to:

(a) Prepare an analysis of production overheads showing the basis of allocation and apportionment to the three departments of the business.

(b) Re-apportion the service department overheads to production departments on the basis of value of machinery.

(c) Calculate an overhead absorption rate based on direct labour hours for each of the two production departments.

(d) Discuss alternative overhead absorption rates that the company could use.

5.5 Mercia Tutorial College has two teaching departments – business studies and general studies – and two service departments – administration and technical support. The overheads of each department are as follows:

	£
• business studies	40,000
• general studies	20,000
• administration	9,600
• technical support	12,000

The basis for re-apportioning the overheads of the service departments is:

• technical support, on the value of equipment in each department – business studies, £50,000; general studies, £25,000; administration, £25,000

• administration, on the number of students in the teaching departments – business studies, 500; general studies, 250

You are to use the step-down method to re-apportion the two service department overheads to the two teaching departments.

5.6 Rossiter and Rossiter is a firm of chartered accountants, with two partners. Overhead costs for next year are estimated to be:

	£
Office rent	10,000
Office salaries	30,000
Rates	4,800
Heating and lighting	2,400
Stationery	2,000
Postage and telephone	5,100
Car expenses	5,600

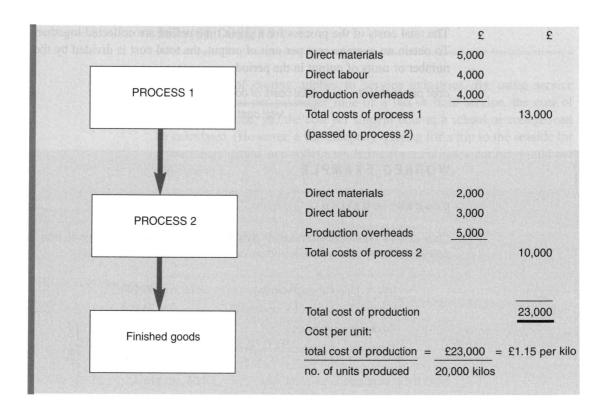

	£	£
Direct materials	5,000	
Direct labour	4,000	
Production overheads	4,000	
Total costs of process 1		13,000
(passed to process 2)		
Direct materials	2,000	
Direct labour	3,000	
Production overheads	5,000	
Total costs of process 2		10,000
Total cost of production		23,000

Cost per unit:

$$\frac{\text{total cost of production}}{\text{no. of units produced}} = \frac{£23,000}{20,000 \text{ kilos}} = £1.15 \text{ per kilo}$$

The book-keeping entries for process costing are explained on pages 162-174.

PROCESS COSTING AND WORK-IN-PROGRESS

Process costing is straightforward if all the items on the production line are completed at the end of the day. In a more complex environment there will be items that have been started but not completed. This is known as **part-finished goods** or **work-in-progress** – see also Chapter 2 (page 38).

For example, the production line at a car factory will always have cars which vary from being only just started, to those nearing the end of the line which are almost complete.

In calculating the cost per unit, it is necessary to take into account the degree of completeness of the part-finished goods. This is done by making equivalent unit calculations:

number of units in progress x percentage of completeness   = equivalent units

Thus, 100 units which are exactly 40% complete are equal to 40 completed units.

The formula for calculating the cost per unit now becomes:

$$\frac{\text{total cost of production}}{\text{number of units of output + equivalent units-in-progress}} = \text{cost per unit}$$

WORKED EXAMPLE

work-in-progress

Cradley Cider Company brews a popular local cider at its cider house in rural Herefordshire. The figures for the first month of the new season's production of its award-winning 'Triple X' variety are:

total cost of production	£8,500
units completed	800 barrels
units in progress	100 barrels

The units in progress are exactly half-finished. The equivalent units in progress, and the cost per barrel, for the month are as follows:

completed units		=	800 barrels
equivalent units	100 x 50%	=	50 barrels
cost per unit	$\frac{£8,500}{800 + 50}$	=	£10 per barrel

Although, in the example above, it was assumed that the work-in-progress was exactly half-finished, this may well not be the case for all the elements of cost. For example, while direct materials might be 100% complete, direct labour, and overheads might be 50% complete. Allowance has to be made for these differences in the calculation of the valuation of work-in-progress, and the layout used in the example below is one way in which the calculations can be made.

WORKED EXAMPLE

work-in-progress

The Toy Manufacturing Company makes a plastic toy called a 'Humber-Wumber'. The figures for the first month's production are:

direct materials	£6,600
direct labour	£3,500
production overheads	£4,000
units completed	900
units in progress	200

The units in progress are complete as regards materials, but are 50% complete for direct labour and overheads.

Cost element	Costs	Completed Units	Work-in-progress			Total Equivalent Units	Cost per Unit	WIP value
			Units	% complete	Equivalent Units			
	A	B	C	D	E	F	G	H
					C x D	B + E	A ÷ F	E x G
	£			%			£	£
Direct materials	6,600	900	200	100	200	1,100	6.00	1,200
Direct labour	3,500	900	200	50	100	1,000	3.50	350
Production overheads	4,000	900	200	50	100	1,000	4.00	400
Total	14,100						13.50	1,950

Note: columns are lettered to show how calculations are made.

Using an average cost basis, the cost per unit of the first month's production, and the month-end valuation figure for work-in-progress (WIP) is as follows:

900 completed units at £13.50 each	=	£12,150
work-in-progress valuation	=	£1,950
total costs for month	=	£14,100

BOOK-KEEPING ENTRIES FOR PROCESS COSTING

In this section we look at the cost book-keeping entries to record process costing transactions. The account to be used is a *process account*, which carries out a similar function to the work-in-progress account that we have used previously.

The basic layout of a process account, which has inputs on the debit side and outputs on the credit side, is shown at the top of the next page.

Dr				Process Account				Cr
	Quantity	Unit cost £	Total £			Quantity	Unit cost £	Total £
Inputs to the process: • transfer from previous process • direct materials • direct labour • direct expenses • production overheads				Outputs from the process: • transfer to next process, or • transfer to finished goods				

Note:

- there are columns for the quantity of goods (eg kilos, litres) input to, and output from, the process
- there are money columns for the unit cost (eg cost per kilo, cost per litre), and for the total
- inputs to the process can include a transfer from a previous process (if any), and any direct costs and production overheads that are added to this stage of the process
- outputs from the process are either a transfer to the next process or, if this is the last or only process, to finished goods stock
- where there is more than one process involved in production, each will have a separate account, eg 'Process 1 Account', 'Process 2 Account'

aspects of process costing

An important feature of process costing is that you don't always get out what you put in to the process. This is illustrated by the example of ordering a steak in a restaurant; the menu will say '250g fillet steak' (explaining that this is the uncooked weight); what comes on the plate will weigh rather less because, when the steak is grilled, fat and liquids are cooked away. Thus, in the 'process' of cooking a steak, the output is less than the input. This is unlike other costing, where the input always equals the output, for example, input the materials for 100 cars, and the output will be 100 cars.

The aspect of process costing where you don't get out what you put in is mainly described as a *normal loss*. This is an unavoidable loss arising from the production process. For example, the normal loss on a 250g steak might be 50g. Normal losses, which occur as a result of factors such as evaporation, breakage, sampling and testing, are included as part of the cost of the output.

Once a standard of normal loss has been established for a process, this then forms the expectation for future processing. Any variation from this normal loss is treated separately in the book-keeping and will be either:

- *abnormal loss*, where the loss is greater than normal, or
- *abnormal gain*, where the loss is less than normal

If any of the losses can be sold as *scrap sales*, the amount of money so received is treated as a reduction in the total costs of the process. Examples include: wood chippings and shavings sold off from wood processing, scrap metal from an engineering company.

With normal loss, abnormal loss, abnormal gain, and scrap sales to consider, there are seven possible outcomes from process costing. These are shown in the following diagram:

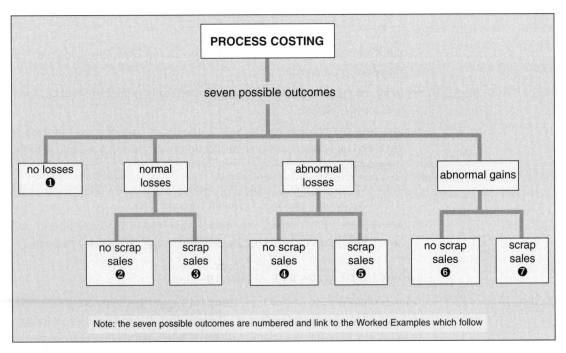

no losses within the process

Here the process account is debited with inputs and credited with the output, which is transferred either to the next process or to finished goods stock.

The cost book-keeping entries are:

- **transfer inputs to the process account**
  - debit process account
  - credit materials, labour, production overhead accounts
- **transfer outputs to the next process or to finished goods stock**
  - debit next process account, or finished goods account
  - credit process account

The cost book-keeping entries are shown diagrammatically as follows:

WORKED EXAMPLE 1

no losses within the process

Garden Eezee Limited manufactures granular fertiliser for use on flowers and vegetables. The fertiliser is made in one production process.

For the four weeks ended 30 January 2007 the company input 11,000 kilos of direct materials and had an output of 11,000 kilos. The input costs were; materials £6,600, labour £3,300, overheads £1,100. There was no opening or closing stock at the beginning and end of the process; all output was complete.

The process cost account for the period is prepared as follows:

Dr				Process Account			Cr
	Quantity	Unit cost	Total		Quantity	Unit cost	Total
	(kilos)	£	£		(kilos)	£	£
Materials	11,000	0.60	6,600	Finished goods	11,000	1.00	11,000
Labour		0.30	3,300	(or to next process)			
Overheads		0.10	1,100				
	11,000		11,000		11,000		11,000

Note: • here the inputs of materials, labour and overheads total £1.00 (60p + 30p + 10p)
  – this figure will be used in subsequent Worked Examples
 • inputs could also include the costs of a previous process

normal losses, with no scrap sales

Here the process account is credited with the expected amount of the normal loss. The amount is recorded in the quantity column only, with no amounts in the money columns. In this way, the cost of the normal loss is included as part of the costs of the output.

WORKED EXAMPLE 2

normal losses, with no scrap sales

Garden Eezee Limited has had to change the chemical composition of its granular fertiliser in order to meet with new European Union regulations. As a result of this, not all of the output can be sold to gardeners. The company's scientists have established that, with an input of 11,000 kilos of raw materials there will be an output of 10,000 kilos and a normal loss of 1,000 kilos.

For the four weeks ended 27 February 2007, the process account is prepared as follows (with the same input costs from Worked Example 1):

Dr				Process Account				Cr
	Quantity	Unit cost	Total		Quantity	Unit cost	Total
	(kilos)	£	£		(kilos)	£	£
Inputs (see	11,000	1.00	11,000	Normal loss	1,000	–	–
Worked Example 1)				Finished goods	10,000	1.10	11,000
				(or to next process)			
	11,000		11,000		11,000		11,000

The cost of the normal losses is included as part of the costs of the output, so the cost per unit is:

$$\frac{\text{input cost}}{\text{expected output}} = \frac{£11,000}{10,000 \text{ kilos}} = £1.10 \text{ per kilo}$$

The cost of the output is transferred to finished goods stock (or to the next process).

normal losses, with scrap sales

If any of the normal losses from a process can be sold – called 'scrap sales' – the process account is credited with the money received. The amount of such sales is recorded in the money column against the normal loss. In this way, the receipts from scrap sales reduce the cost of the output.

WORKED EXAMPLE 3

normal losses, with scrap sales

Garden Eezee Limited is now able to sell its normal losses to a specialist reprocessing company. The price it receives for the scrap sales is 50p per kilo.

For the four weeks ended 26 March 2007 the process account is prepared as follows (with the same input costs and normal loss as Worked Example 2):

Dr				Process Account			Cr
	Quantity	Unit cost	Total		Quantity	Unit cost	Total
	(kilos)	£	£		(kilos)	£	£
Inputs	11,000	1.00	11,000	Normal loss	1,000	–	500
				(scrap sales)			
				Finished goods	10,000	1.05	10,500
				(or to next process)			
	11,000		11,000		11,000		11,000

The value of the scrap sales reduces the cost per unit of the expected output to:

$$\frac{\text{input cost} - \text{scrap value of normal loss}}{\text{expected output}} \quad = \quad \frac{£11,000 - £500}{10,000 \text{ kilos}}$$

$$= \text{£1.05 per kilo}$$

Normal loss account is debited with £500 by transfer from the process account. The receipts from scrap sales are then credited to this account and debited to either bank account (cash received), or debtor's account (sold on credit terms). Normal loss account then appears as:

Dr		Normal Loss Account		Cr
	£			£
Process account	500	Bank/debtors		500

7 Book-keeping for costing

this chapter covers . . .

This chapter explains:

- the use of
    - a manufacturing account to show production cost
    - a profit and loss account to show net profit
- the importance of identification and coding of costs
- how an integrated book-keeping system incorporates the accounts for both costing and financial accounting
- the book-keeping to record under-absorption and over-absorption of overheads
- the book-keeping entries for process costing

PERFORMANCE CRITERIA COVERED

unit 6: RECORDING AND ANALYSNG COSTS AND REVENUES

element 6.1

record and analyse information relating to direct costs and revenues

A   identify direct costs in accordance with the organisation's costing procedures

B   record and analyse information relating to direct costs

C   calculate direct costs in accordance with the organisation's policies and procedures

element 6.2

record and analyse information relating to the allocation, apportionment and

absorption of overhead costs

D   record and analyse information relating to overhead costs in accordance with the organisation's procedures

E   make adjustments for under and over recovered overhead costs in accordance with established procedures

THE USE OF A MANUFACTURING ACCOUNT

As we saw in Chapter 1, a business brings together all of the costs involved in producing its output in the form of a *total cost statement:*

		£
	Direct materials	x
add	Direct labour	x
add	Direct expenses	x
equals	PRIME COST	x
add	Production overheads	x
equals	PRODUCTION COST	x
add	Non-production overheads, eg	
	• selling and distribution expenses	x
	• administration expenses	x
	• finance expenses	x
equals	TOTAL COST	x

A total cost statement can be prepared on the basis of a single cost unit, or a batch, or a whole production unit such as a factory. However, overall, a business needs to have an accounting system that records its costs and its sales for all its output, and then shows the profit or loss that has been made for the accounting period. For a business such as a retailer that buys and sells goods, without carrying out any production processes, the accounting system is relatively simple – the figure for sales is deducted from the amount of purchases (after allowing for changes in the value of opening and closing stock) and the amount of overheads; a profit is made when sales exceed the total costs. For a manufacturer, though, the costs are more complex as they comprise the direct and indirect costs of materials, labour and expenses; also, a manufacturer will invariably have opening and closing stock in three different forms – direct materials, work-in-progress and finished goods.

In its year-end (or final) accounts a manufacturer uses the layout of the total cost statement and prepares:

• a manufacturing account, which shows production cost

• a profit and loss account, which shows net profit for the accounting period

The final accounts use the following outline:

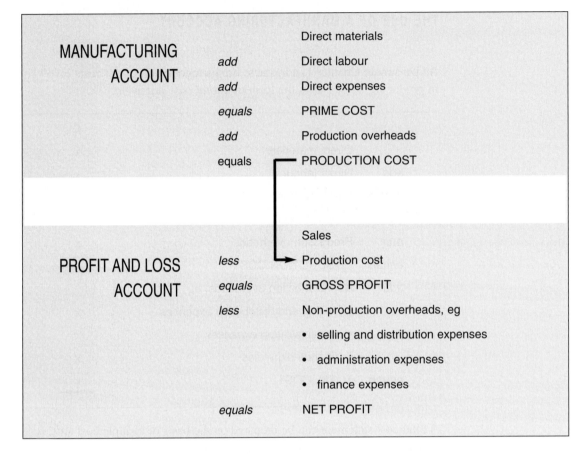

notes

- Adjustments have to be made to allow for changes in the value of stock at the start of the accounting period (opening stock) and at the end of the accounting period (closing stock) for:
    - direct materials, in the manufacturing account
    - work-in-progress (or partly manufactured goods), in the manufacturing account
    - finished goods, in the profit and loss account
- The profit and loss account shows two levels of profit:
    - gross profit, the difference between selling price and production cost (after allowing for changes in the value of opening and closing stock)
    - net profit, the profit after all costs have been deducted and which belongs to the owner(s) of the business
- Certain expenses might be apportioned on an appropriate basis between the manufacturing account and the profit and loss account – for example, rent and rates might be apportioned 75 per cent to the factory (production overheads) and 25 per cent to the office (non-production overheads)

An example of a manufacturing and profit and loss account is shown below:

ALPHA MANUFACTURING COMPANY
MANUFACTURING AND PROFIT AND LOSS ACCOUNT
for the year ended 31 December 2007

	£	£
Opening stock of direct materials		5,000
Add Purchases of direct materials		50,000
		55,000
Less Closing stock of direct materials		6,000
COST OF DIRECT MATERIALS USED		49,000
Direct labour		26,000
Direct expenses		2,500
PRIME COST		77,500
Add Production (factory) overheads:		
Indirect materials	2,000	
Indirect labour	16,000	
Indirect expenses:		
Rent of factory	5,000	
Depreciation of factory machinery	10,000	
Factory light and heat	4,000	
		37,000
		114,500
Add Opening stock of work-in-progress		4,000
		118,500
Less Closing stock of work-in-progress		3,000
PRODUCTION COST OF GOODS COMPLETED		115,500
Sales		195,500
Opening stock of finished goods	6,500	
Production cost of goods completed	115,500	
	122,000	
Less Closing stock of finished goods	7,500	
COST OF SALES		114,500
Gross profit		81,000
Less Non-production overheads:		
Selling and distribution expenses	38,500	
Administration expenses	32,000	
Finance expenses	3,500	
		74,000
Net profit		7,000

IDENTIFICATION AND CODING OF COSTS

In order to be able to prepare the final accounts of manufacturing account and profit and loss account, a business must use a detailed book-keeping system which enables accurate information to be extracted. For the book-keeping system to be accurate, as costs are incurred they must be charged to the correct account in the system. This is achieved by a system of:

- identification of the cost unit or cost centre to which the cost is to be charged
- coding the cost so that it is charged to the correct book-keeping account of the cost unit or cost centre

Systems of coding have been discussed earlier (page 14). Here we are concerned with the place of the coding system as a part of the book-keeping process. This is illustrated as follows:

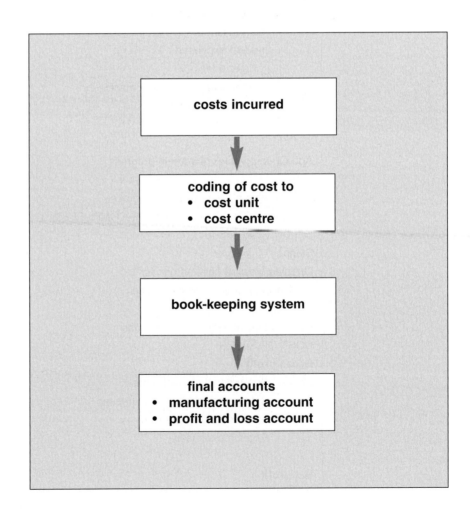

INTEGRATED BOOK-KEEPING SYSTEM

This section brings together the double-entry accounts which record transactions about the cost of a product or service, and the sales revenues. Such an *integrated book-keeping system* incorporates the accounts of the business for both costing and financial accounting, ie the book-keeping for the two types of accounting is combined together in one ledger rather than being kept in separate, non-integrated, ledgers. We have already seen the book-keeping entries for various aspects of the costing system:

- for materials, Chapter 2 (pages 61-65)
- for labour, Chapter 3 (pages 82-85)
- for expenses, Chapter 4 (pages 98-99)
- for overheads, Chapter 5 (pages 133-136)

Here we look at how these are integrated into the book-keeping system. Always remember the principles of double-entry book-keeping that are to be followed:

- a debit entry records a gain in value, an asset or an expense
- a credit entry records the giving of value, a liability or an income item

We will see how an integrated book-keeping system is used by considering three separate stages:

> stage 1 – manufacturing costs and profit and loss account
>
> stage 2 – direct and indirect costs
>
> stage 3 – receipts and payments

Using the diagram on the next page, we will focus on each of the three stages.

stage 1 – manufacturing costs and profit and loss account (on the right-hand side of the diagram)

- this stage incorporates the manufacturing costs of direct materials, direct labour, direct expenses (if any), and production overheads
- these costs are debited to work-in-progress account
- from work-in-progress account the cost of those goods that are completed is transferred to finished goods account
- cost of sales is the manufacturing cost of those goods that have been sold
- profit and loss account incorporates the non-production overheads
- profit is sales minus cost of sales and non-production overheads
- transfers out of materials, work-in-progress and finished goods are for the amount taken to the next stage of production; for example, with

continued on page 187

THE INTEGRATED BOOK-KEEPING SYSTEM

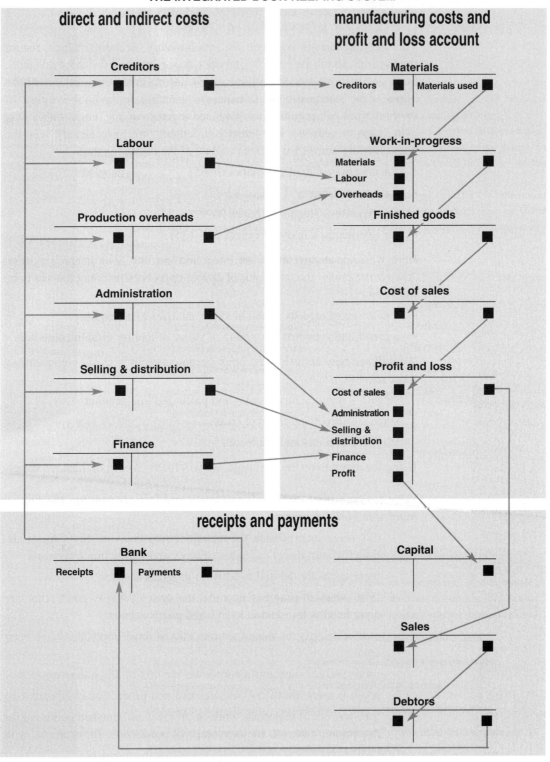

materials, only those materials used in production will be transferred to work-in-progress – any balance remaining on materials account represents the stock held at the end of the accounting period

stage 2 – direct and indirect costs (on the left-hand side of the diagram)

- this shows how the direct and indirect costs are built up on the debit side of each account
- amounts are then transferred to manufacturing costs and profit and loss account

stage 3 – receipts and payments (at the bottom of the diagram)

- here profit for the accounting period is transferred to capital
- the sales account is linked to profit and loss account and to the debtors' accounts
- receipts from debtors are debited in bank account
- payments are made from bank account to settle creditors and the direct and indirect costs of the business, so completing the book-keeping 'loop'

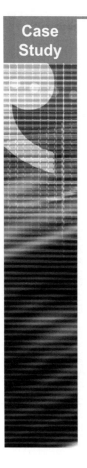

Case Study

MARTLEY MANUFACTURING: INTEGRATED BOOK-KEEPING SYSTEM

situation

Martley Manufacturing started in business making wooden toys on 1 January 2007. During January the following transactions took place:

	£
Opening capital paid in to bank	10,000
Direct materials bought on credit	5,000
Direct labour costs paid by cheque	6,000
Production overheads paid by cheque	3,000
Non-production overheads paid by cheque	2,000
Credit sales	15,000
Receipts from debtors	12,000
Payments to creditors	3,500
Direct materials transferred to work-in-progress	4,000
Work-in-progress transferred to finished goods	11,000
Finished goods transferred to cost of sales	10,000

The above transactions are to be recorded in the integrated book-keeping system of Martley Manufacturing. Note that:

- the full cost of direct labour is to be transferred to work-in-progress
- there are no direct expenses
- the full cost of production overheads is to be transferred to work-in-progress

solution

It is suggested that you 'audit' the month's transactions to the double-entry accounts; in particular, ensure that you can understand the debit and credit entry for each transaction.

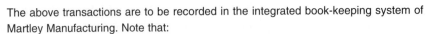

STAGE 1: MANUFACTURING COSTS AND PROFIT AND LOSS ACCOUNT

Dr		**Materials Account**		Cr
	£			£
Creditors	5,000	Work-in-progress		4,000
		Balance c/d		1,000
	5,000			5,000
Balance b/d	1,000			

Dr		**Work-in-Progress Account**		Cr
	£			£
Direct materials	4,000	Finished goods		11,000
Direct labour	6,000	Balance c/d		2,000
Production overhead	3,000			
	13,000			13,000
Balance b/d	2,000			

Dr		**Finished Goods Account**		Cr
	£			£
Work-in-progress	11,000	Cost of sales		10,000
		Balance c/d		1,000
	11,000			11,000
Balance b/d	1,000			

Dr		**Cost of Sales Account**		Cr
	£			£
Finished goods	10,000	Profit and loss		10,000

Dr	**Profit and Loss Account**		Cr
	£		£
Cost of sales	10,000	Sales	15,000
Non-production overhead	2,000		
Net profit (to capital account)	3,000		
	15,000		15,000

STAGE 2: DIRECT AND INDIRECT COSTS

Dr	**Creditors' Account**		Cr
	£		£
Bank	3,500	Materials	5,000
Balance c/d	1,500		
	5,000		5,000
		Balance b/d	1,500

Dr	**Labour Costs Account**		Cr
	£		£
Bank	6,000	Work-in-progress	6,000

Dr	**Production Overheads Account**		Cr
	£		£
Bank	3,000	Work-in-progress	3,000

Dr	**Non-Production Overheads Account**		Cr
	£		£
Bank	2,000	Profit and loss	2,000

STAGE 3: RECEIPTS AND PAYMENTS

Dr		**Capital Account**		Cr
	£			£
Balance c/d	13,000	Bank		10,000
		Profit and loss		3,000
	13,000			13,000
		Balance b/d		13,000

Dr		**Sales Account**		Cr
	£			£
Profit and loss	15,000	Debtors		15,000

Dr		**Debtors Account**		Cr
	£			£
Sales	15,000	Bank		12,000
		Balance c/d		3,000
	15,000			15,000
Balance b/d	3,000			

Dr		**Bank Account**		Cr
	£			£
Capital	10,000	Creditors		3,500
Debtors	12,000	Labour		6,000
		Production overheads		3,000
		Non-production overheads		2,000
		Balance c/d		7,500
	22,000			22,000
Balance b/d	7,500			

In bank account the transactions have been listed in the order in which they appear in the book-keeping, and are not necessarily in chronological order.

Note the following points:

- At the end of January the book-keeping system balances, as shown by the following trial balance:

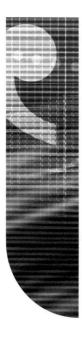

	Dr	Cr
	£	£
Materials	1,000	
Work-in-progress	2,000	
Finished goods	1,000	
Creditors		1,500
Capital		13,000
Debtors	3,000	
Bank	7,500	
	14,500	14,500

- As the business has stocks of materials, work-in-progress and raw materials at the end of the month, transfers from the accounts to the next stage of production are reduced; the balance remaining on each account shows the value of the stock at the end of the month.

- For simplicity, control accounts have not been used. An example of a wages control account is shown in Chapter 3, page 85.

OVERHEADS: UNDER-ABSORPTION AND OVER-ABSORPTION

In Chapter 5, we saw that businesses and other organisations often set pre-determined overhead rates for production overheads. Differences may occur between the pre-determined rate and the actual amount of overhead absorbed into the cost units because of a combination of:

- actual output differing from expected output
- actual costs incurred differing from expected costs

Thus it is common for overhead to be either under-absorbed, or over-absorbed:

- with under-absorption the overheads absorbed into the cost units are less than the overheads actually incurred
- with over-absorption the overheads absorbed into the cost units are more than the overheads actually incurred

Under-absorbed overhead is debited to profit and loss account, where it adds to costs and reduces profit; over-absorbed overhead is credited to profit and loss account, where it increases profit. Remember that neither excessive under- or over-absorption of overheads is desirable; they are an indication that the product has been costed inaccurately, which is likely to mean that the selling price has been calculated either too low (under-absorption) or too high (over-absorption).

For non-production overheads, there are no under-absorption or over-absorption amounts. This is because non-production overheads are not part of production cost; instead their costs are debited directly to profit and loss account.

The Case Study which follows summarises the book-keeping entries for overheads. These are also covered in Chapter 5 (pages 133-136).

Case Study

UNDER-ABSORPTION AND OVER-ABSORPTION OF OVERHEADS: DEPARTMENTS A AND B

DEPARTMENT A

situation

• overhead absorption rate is £2.00 per direct labour hour
• direct labour hours worked in March were 2,000
• actual cost of production overhead in March was £4,500

solution

• overhead absorbed by cost units £2.00 x 2,000 hours	=	£4,000
• actual cost of production overhead	=	£4,500
• under-absorption of overhead	=	£500

The work-in-progress account is charged with production overheads of £4,000; however, this will leave a debit balance of £500 on production overheads account. This amount is transferred to profit and loss account as follows:

• debit profit and loss account
• credit production overheads account

Production overheads account appears as follows:

Dr	**Production Overheads Account: Department A**		Cr
	£		£
Bank (overheads incurred)	4,500	Work-in-progress	4,000
		Profit and loss (under-absorption)	500
	4,500		4,500

The amount of under-absorbed overhead adds to the total costs of the business, and so reduces profits.

There was no work-in-progress at either the beginning or end of the week.

Output during the week was 1,400 kilos from Process 1 and 4,200 kilos from Process 2.

As an accounts assistant at Perran Chemicals Limited you are asked to prepare the process 1 account, process 2 account, normal loss account, abnormal loss account, and abnormal gain account for the week ended 14 May 2007. Note: calculate costs per unit of expected output to the nearest penny.

solution

Dr	Quantity (kilos)	Unit cost £	Total £	**Process 1 Account**	Quantity (kilos)	Unit cost £	Total £	Cr
Materials	2,000	4.00	8,000	Normal loss (20%)	400	–	400	
Labour			720	Transfer to process 2	1,400	6.10	8,540	
Overheads			1,440	Abnormal loss	200	6.10	1,220	
	2,000		10,160		2,000		10,160	

Dr	Quantity (kilos)	Unit cost £	Total £	**Process 2 Account**	Quantity (kilos)	Unit cost £	Total £	Cr
Transfer from process 1	1,400	6.10	8,540	Normal loss (10%)	450	–	450	
Materials	3,100	6.00	18,600	Finished goods	4,200	6.95	29,172	
Labour			960					
Overheads			480					
	4,500		28,580					
Abnormal gain	150	6.95	1,042					
	4,650		29,622		4,650		29,622	

Dr	£	**Normal Loss Account**	£	Cr
Process 1 account	400	Bank/debtors	400	
Process 2 account	450	Abnormal gain account	*150	
		Bank/debtors	300	
	850		850	

* see abnormal gain account

Dr		Abnormal Loss Account	Cr
	£		£
Process 1 account	1,220	Bank/debtors (200 kilos x £1.00)	200

Dr		Abnormal Gain Account	Cr
	£		£
Normal loss account	*150	Process 2 account	1,042
* 150 kilos x £1.00 per kilo			

Tutorial notes:

- In process 1, the cost per unit of expected output is:

$$\frac{£10,160 - £400}{1,600 \text{ kilos*}} = £6.10 \text{ per kilo}$$

   * ie 2,000 kilos x 80%

- In process 2, the cost per unit of expected output is:

$$\frac{£28,580 - £450}{4,050 \text{ kilos**}} = £6.95 \text{ per kilo}$$

   ** ie 4,500 kilos x 90%

- At the end of the financial year:

   – the balance of abnormal loss account, here £1,020 (ie £1,220 – £200), is debited to profit and loss account

   – the balance of abnormal gain account, here £892 (ie £1,042 – £150), is credited to profit and loss account

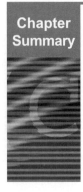

Chapter Summary

- A manufacturing account shows prime cost and production cost.

- Profit and loss account shows non-production overheads and the net profit of the business.

- Correct identification and coding of costs is important in the preparation of accurate final accounts.

- An integrated book-keeping system incorporates the accounts of the business for both costing and financial accounting.

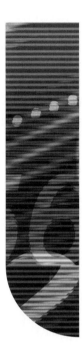

- Under- or over-absorption of overheads affects profit:
  - under-absorbed overhead is debited to profit and loss account, so reducing profit
  - over-absorbed overhead is credited to profit and loss account, so increasing profit
- Book-keeping for process costing uses a process account to calculate the cost per unit of expected output. Possible outcomes of process costing to be recorded in the accounts are:
  - no losses within the process
  - normal losses, with or without scrap sales
  - abnormal losses, with or without scrap sales
  - abnormal gains, with or without scrap sales

  At the end of a financial year, the balance of abnormal loss account is debited to profit and loss account, while the balance of abnormal gain account is credited

Key Terms

manufacturing account	double-entry account which brings together all the elements of cost that make up production cost
integrated book-keeping	combines the accounts for costing and financial accounting
under-absorption of overheads	where overheads absorbed into the cost units are less than the overheads actually incurred; profit is reduced
over-absorption of overheads	where overheads absorbed into the cost units are more than the overheads actually incurred; profit is increased
process account	account which is used to calculate the cost per unit of expected output; it is: – debited with the cost of inputs (materials, labour and overheads) – credited with the transfer to the next process or to finished goods
normal loss account	account used in process costing which is – debited with the scrap sales value of normal losses – credited with receipts from scrap sales

abnormal loss account	account used in process costing which is
	– debited with the value of abnormal losses (at a cost per unit value of the expected output)
	– credited with receipts from scrap sales
abnormal gain account	account used in process costing which is
	– debited with the equivalent value of scrap sales for normal losses
	– credited with the value of abnormal gains (at a cost per unit value of the expected output)

Student Activities

7.1 Which one of the following does not appear in a manufacturing account?

(a) depreciation of factory machinery

(b) indirect labour

(c) depreciation of office equipment

(d) factory light and heat

Answer (a) or (b) or (c) or (d)

7.2 For a manufacturing business, which type of stock is recorded in the profit and loss account?

(a) raw materials

(b) work-in-progress

(c) partly manufactured goods

(d) finished goods

Answer (a) or (b) or (c) or (d)

SHORT-TERM DECISIONS

what is meant by short-term decisions?

By short-term decisions we mean those actions which will affect the costs and revenues of a business or organisation over the next few weeks and months, up to a maximum of one year ahead. Long-term decisions – see Chapter 9 – affect the costs and revenues of future years. For example, an ice-cream manufacturer might make the following decisions:

- *short-term* – 'we have to increase production over the summer months in order to meet higher sales'

- *long-term* – 'we need to build a production line so that we can make the new Veneto range of ice creams that we are developing.'

types of short-term decisions

The decisions that we will be looking at include:

- Break-even analysis, where the break-even point is the output level (units manufactured or services provided) at which the income from sales is just enough to cover all the costs. Break-even analysis answers questions such as:
  - what output do we need in order to break-even?
  - at current levels of output we are above break-even, but how safe are we?
  - we have to make a profit of £1,000 per week; what level of output do we need to achieve this?
  - what is the effect on profit if we sell more or less than we think?

- Limiting factors, where there is a shortage which affects output. Limiting factors include a shortage of materials, skilled labour, machine hours, etc. Once the limiting factor has been identified, the effect of the constraint on output can be minimised in order to achieve the best results for the business or organisation. A knowledge of limiting factors answers questions such as:
  - there is a shortage of materials this week – shall we produce Product Exe or Product Wye?
  - until we complete the training programme we have a shortage of skilled labour; how best can we use the skilled labour that we have available?
  - one of the machines has broken down; both of our products need machine hours – which product takes priority?

- Marginal costing identifies the fixed and variable costs that are required to make a product or to provide a service. Once these are known questions about pricing can be answered:

- if we increase prices, sales are expected to fall but how will our profit be affected?
- if we decrease prices, sales are expected to increase but how will our profit be affected?
- a potential customer wants to buy our product but at a lower price than we usually charge; how will our profit be affected?

what information is needed?

Decision-making, both in the short-term and long-term, is concerned with the future and always involves making a choice between alternatives. To help with decision-making it is important to identify the *relevant costs*.

Relevant costs are those costs that are appropriate to a particular decision.

In order to make a decision, information is needed about costs and revenues:

- future costs and revenues
  - it is the expected future costs and revenues that are important
  - past costs and revenues are only useful in so far as they provide a guide to the future
  - costs already spent (called *sunk costs*) are irrelevant to decision-making
- differential costs and revenues
  - only those costs which alter as a result of decision-making are relevant
  - where costs are the same for each alternative, they are irrelevant
  - thus any cost that changes when a decision is made is a relevant cost

In the short-term, a business or organisation always attempts to make the best use of existing resources. This involves focusing on what will change as a result of a decision being made, such as:

- selling prices
- variable costs
- contribution per unit of output, which is selling price minus variable cost
- marginal cost, which is the cost of producing one extra unit of output

Typically, fixed costs do not alter in short-term decision-making, eg the rent of a car factory is most likely to be the same when 11,000 cars are produced each year instead of 10,000 previously.

reporting decisions

With decision-making – both short- and long-term – the costing information has to be reported to managers, or other appropriate people, in a clear and concise way. The information should include recommendations which are supported by well-presented reasoning. The decisions will not be taken by the person who has prepared the information, but the decision-makers will be influenced by the recommendations of the report. Remember that managers, and other appropriate people, do not always have an accounting background, so any form of presentation must be set out clearly and must use as little technical accounting terminology as possible.

Methods of presentation include:

• verbal presentations

• written reports/memorandums

Both of these require a similar amount of preparation; the steps are:

– plan the report

– check that the plan deals with the tasks set

– be aware of the context in which the report is written

– make sure all work is legible

– express the report, verbal or written, in clear and concise English

written reports

The written report should include:

– an introduction, which sets out the task or the problem

– the content of the report, which explains the steps towards a solution and may include accounting calculations

– a conclusion, which includes a recommendation of the decision to be taken

– an appendix, which can be used to explain fully the accounting calculations, and to detail any sources of reference consulted

In this chapter we will see two written reports on short-term decisions which make recommendations – see pages 224 and 232. The next chapter includes an example of a report for a long-term decision.

verbal presentations

A verbal presentation requires the same preparation and content as a written report and is probably the more difficult to present. Accordingly, verbal presentations often include support material in the form of handouts, overhead projector transparencies, or computer displays linked to an overhead projector. Such material can be used to explain accounting data and to make key points and recommendations.

FIXED AND VARIABLE COSTS

Before we can look at short-term decision-making techniques, it is important to understand that costs behave in different ways as the volume of output or activity changes. We have already seen (Chapter 4, pages 100-103) that there are three ways in which costs can behave within a range of output levels. These are summarised as follows:

variable costs   These are the costs where the the cost varies in proportion to the level of output. For example, if a car manufacturer makes more cars it will use more sheet metal – a variable cost.

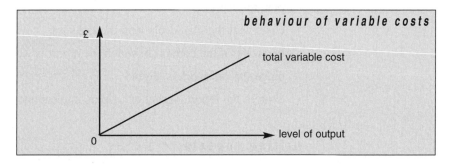

fixed costs   These are costs that do not normally change when the level of output changes. The cost of insuring a car factory against business risks will not vary in line with the number of cars produced – it is a fixed cost.

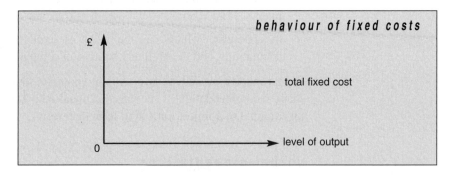

Remember that increases in output may produce a stepped fixed cost, eg an increase in factory rent because an additional factory is needed for the increase in output. The nature of stepped fixed costs is illustrated on page 101.

semi-variable costs These are costs where a part of the cost acts as a variable cost, and a part acts as a fixed cost. Some fuel bills are semi-variable: there is a fixed 'standing charge' and a variable 'unit charge'.

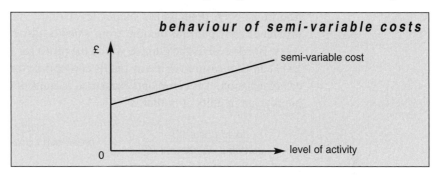

costs, contribution and profit

To help with decision-making, costs are classifed as either variable costs or fixed costs (semi-variable costs are divided into their fixed and variable components). For example, a car manufacturer will need to identify:

- the variable costs of each car

- the total fixed costs of running the business over a period of time

When the manufacturer sells a car it receives the selling price, which covers the variable costs of the car. As the selling price is greater than the variable costs there will also be money available to pay off the fixed costs incurred. This amount of money is known as the **contribution**. The formula is:

selling price per unit *less* variable cost per unit = contribution per unit

It follows that the difference between the sales income and the variable costs of the units sold in a period is the **total contribution** that the sales of all the units in the period make towards the fixed costs of the organisation.

A business can work out its profit for any given period from the total contribution and fixed costs figures:

total contribution *less* total fixed costs = profit

A profit statement can be prepared in the following format:

	sales revenue
less	variable costs
equals	contribution
less	fixed costs
equals	profit

BREAK-EVEN

Break-even is the point at which neither a profit nor a loss is made.

The break-even point is the output level (units manufactured or services provided) at which the income from sales is just enough to cover all the costs. Break-even is the point at which the profit (or loss) is zero. The output level can be measured in a way that is appropriate for the particular business or organisation. It is commonly measured in units of output. The formula for break-even in units of output is:

$$\frac{\text{fixed costs (£)}}{\text{contribution per unit (£)}} = \text{break-even point (in units of output)}$$

In order to use break-even analysis, we need to know:

- selling price (per unit)
- costs of the product
  - variable costs (such as materials, labour) per unit
  - overhead costs, and whether these are fixed or variable
- limitations, such as maximum production capacity, maximum sales

The Case Study of Fluffy Toys Limited which follows shows how the break-even point can be worked out.

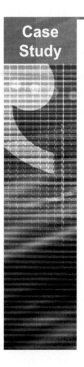

Case Study

FLUFFY TOYS LIMITED: BREAK-EVEN

situation

Fluffy Toys Limited manufactures soft toys, and is able to sell all that can be produced. The variable costs (materials and direct labour) for producing each toy are £10 and the selling price is £20 each. The fixed costs of running the business are £5,000 per month. How many toys need to be produced and sold each month for the business to cover its costs, ie to break-even?

solution

This problem can be solved by calculation, by constructing a table, or by means of a graph. Which method is used depends on the purpose for which the information is required:

- the *calculation method* is quick to use and is convenient for seeing the effect of different cost structures on break-even point

- the *table method* shows the amounts of fixed and variable costs, sales revenue, and profit at different levels of production

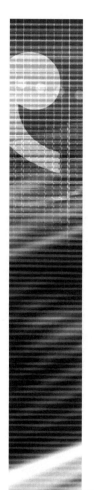

- the *graph method* is used for making presentations – for example, to the directors of a company – because it shows in a visual form the relationship between costs and sales revenue, and the amount of profit or loss at different levels of production

Often the calculation or table methods are used before drawing a graph. By doing this, the break-even point is known and suitable scales can be selected for the axes of the graph in order to give a good visual presentation.

calculation method

The contribution per unit is:

	selling price per unit	£20
less	variable costs per unit	£10
equals	contribution per unit	£10

Each toy sold gives a contribution (selling price, less variable costs) of £10. This contributes towards the fixed costs and, in order to break-even, the business must have sufficient £10 'lots' to meet the fixed costs. Thus, with fixed costs of £5,000 per month, the break-even calculation is:

$$\frac{fixed\ costs\ (£)}{contribution\ per\ unit\ (£)} \ = \ \frac{£5,000}{£10} \ = \ 500\ toys\ each\ month$$

The break-even point (in units of output) is 500 toys each month.

table method

units of output	fixed costs	variable costs	total cost	sales revenue	profit/(loss)
	A	B	C	D	
			A + B		D – C
	£	£	£	£	£
100	5,000	1,000	6,000	2,000	(4,000)
200	5,000	2,000	7,000	4,000	(3,000)
300	5,000	3,000	8,000	6,000	(2 000)
400	5,000	4,000	9,000	8,000	(1,000)
500	5,000	5,000	10,000	10,000	nil
600	5,000	6,000	11,000	12,000	1,000
700	5,000	7,000	12,000	14,000	2,000

graph method

A graphical presentation uses money amounts as the common denominator between fixed costs, variable costs, and sales revenue.

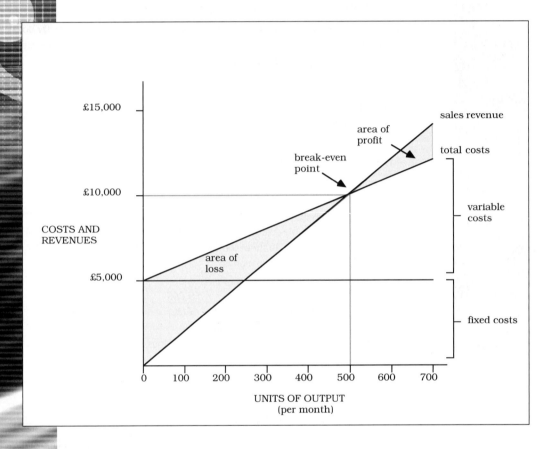

notes to the graph

- With a break-even graph, it is usual for the vertical axis to show money amounts; the horizontal axis shows units of output/sales.

- The fixed costs are unchanged at all levels of output, in this case they are £5,000.

- The variable costs commence, on the vertical axis, *from the fixed costs amount*, not from 'zero'. This is because the cost of producing zero units is the fixed costs.

- The fixed costs *and* the variable costs form the *total costs line*.

- The point at which the total costs and sales revenue lines cross is the break-even point.

- From the graph we can read off the break-even point both in terms of units of output, 500 units on the horizontal axis, and in sales value, £10,000 on the vertical axis.

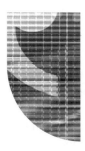

- The 'proof' of the break-even chart is:

		£
	sales revenue (500 units at £20 each)	10,000
less	variable costs (500 units at £10 each)	5,000
equals	contribution	5,000
less	fixed costs	5,000
equals	profit/loss	nil

HINTS FOR DRAWING A BREAK-EVEN GRAPH

> **Tutorial note**: It is unlikely that you will be asked to draw a break-even graph in an Examination for *Recording and Analysing Costs and Revenues*. Nevertheless, it is good practice and illustrates well the relationship between costs and revenues.

- In most break-even charts *all lines are straight.* This means that only two points need be plotted for each line; for example, with sales, choose a number that is fairly near to the maximum expected, multiply by the selling price per unit, and this is the point to be marked on the graph. As the sales line always passes through zero, there are now two points along which to draw a straight line.

- When drawing a break-even graph it is often difficult to know what total value to show on each axis, ie how many units, and/or how much in costs and revenues. As a guide, look for a maximum output or sales level that will not be exceeded: this will give the horizontal axis. Multiply the maximum sales, if known, by the unit selling price to give the maximum sales revenue for the vertical axis. If the figure for maximum sales is not known, it is recommended that the break-even point is calculated before drawing the graph so that the extent of the graph can be established.

- A common error is to start the variable costs from the zero point instead of the fixed costs line.

- Although fixed costs are likely to be unchanged within a fairly narrow range of outputs, watch out for *stepped fixed costs* (see page 101). For example, a major expansion of output may require that additional premises are rented: thus the fixed cost of rent will increase at a particular point (and is shown graphically as a step). Such a stepped fixed cost has a direct effect on total costs.

INTERPRETATION OF BREAK-EVEN

When interpreting break-even, it is all too easy to concentrate solely on the break-even point. The graph, for example, tells us much more than this: it also shows the profit or loss at any level of output/sales contained within the graph. To find this, simply measure the gap between sales revenue and total costs at a chosen number of units, and read the money amounts off on the vertical axis (above break-even point it is a profit; below, it is a loss). For example, the graph in the Case Study above shows a profit or loss at:

• 650 units = £1,500 profit

• 600 units = £1,000 profit

• 400 units = £1,000 loss

Break-even analysis, whether by calculation, by table, or by graph, can be used by all types of businesses and organistions. For example, a shop will wish to know the sales it has to make each week to meet costs; a sports centre will wish to know the ticket sales that have to be made to meet costs; a club or society might wish to know how many raffle tickets it needs to sell to meet the costs of prizes and of printing tickets.

Once the break-even point has been reached, the *additional* contribution forms the profit. For example, if the business considered in the Case Study above was selling 650 toys each month, it would have a total contribution of 650 x £10 = £6,500; of this the first £5,000 will be used to meet fixed costs, and the remaining £1,500 represents the profit (which can be read off the break-even graph). This can be shown by means of a profit statement as follows:

		£
	sales revenue (650 units at £20 each)	13,000
less	variable costs (650 units at £10 each)	6,500
equals	contribution (to fixed costs and profit)	6,500
less	monthly fixed costs	5,000
equals	profit for month	1,500

LIMITATIONS OF BREAK-EVEN ANALYSIS

The problem of break-even analysis is the assumption that the relationship between sales revenue, variable costs and fixed costs, remains the same at all levels of production. This is a rather simplistic view because, for example, in order to increase sales, a business will often need to offer bulk discounts, so reducing the sales revenue per unit at higher levels. The limitations of break-even analysis can be summarised as follows:

- The assumption is made that all output is sold. There is no point in preparing the cost data, calculating the break-even point, and estimating the profits to be made if the product will not sell in sufficient quantities. However, break-even analysis is useful for a new business in order to establish the level of sales that must be achieved to reach break-even point. The feasibility of reaching that level of sales must then be considered by the owners.

- All costs and revenues are expressed in terms of straight lines. However, this relationship is not always so. As indicated above selling prices may vary at different quantities sold; in a similar way, as we have seen earlier in the chapter, variable costs alter at different levels as advantage is taken of the lower prices to be gained from bulk buying, and/or more efficient production methods.

- Fixed costs do not remain fixed at all levels of production; instead, as we have seen, there may be stepped fixed costs.

- It is not possible to *extrapolate* the graph or calculation; by extrapolation is meant extending the lines on the graph beyond the limits of the activity on which the graph is based. For example, in the Case Study, the graph cannot be extended to, say, 1,000 units of output and the profit read off at this point. The relationship between sales revenues and costs will be different at much higher levels of output – different methods of production might be used, for example.

- The profit or loss shown by the graph or calculations is probably only true for figures close to current output levels – the further away from current figures, the less accurate will be the expected profit or loss.

- A further disadvantage of break-even analysis is that it concentrates too much attention on the break-even point. While this aspect is important, other considerations such as ensuring that the output is produced as efficiently as possible, and that costs are kept under review, are just as important.

BREAK-EVEN: MARGIN OF SAFETY

The margin of safety is the amount by which sales exceed the break-even point. Margin of safety can be expressed as:

- a number of units
- a sales revenue amount

Report for managing director:

REPORT

To: Managing Director

From: Accounts Assistant

Date: Today

Production of Windsor and Buckingham models

Introduction

- You asked for my recommendations for next week's production.

- Until we have completed the training of new employees, the company has insufficient skilled labour to enable us to manufacture both models to meet customer demand. We therefore need to use our skilled labour to the best advantage of the company.

Report

- With insufficient skilled labour we have a limiting factor (or a scarce resource). To make best use of this limiting factor to produce profits for the company, we must maximise the contribution (selling price – variable costs) from each hour of skilled labour.

- The contribution from producing each Windsor radio is £20. As this product requires two hours of skilled labour, the contribution per hour is £20 ÷ 2 hours = £10.

- The contribution from producing each Buckingham radio is £30. As this product also requires two hours of skilled labour, the contribution per hour is £30 ÷ 2 hours = £15.

- To make best use of the limiting factor of skilled labour, the company should produce all of the Buckingham model that can be sold, io 80 per week. This will take 160 hours of skilled labour (80 radios x 2 hours each) and will leave 100 hours available to produce 50 of the Windsor model (50 radios x 2 hours each).

- Please note that, if this production plan is followed, insufficient Windsor models will be produced to meet demand. This may make it difficult to re-establish the Windsor in the market when full production of this model can be resumed following the completion of training of new employees.

Conclusion

- Based on the concept of maximising the contribution from each hour of skilled labour (the limiting factor), I recommend that the production for next week should be:

    80 Buckingham radios

    50 Windsor radios

continued on next page

- This will give a forecast profit statement for next week as follows:

		Windsor £	Buckingham £	Total £
	Sales revenue:			
	50 Windsor at £50 per unit	2,500		2,500
	80 Buckingham at £100 per unit		8,000	8,000
		2,500	8,000	10,500
less	Variable costs:			
	50 Windsor at £30 per unit	1,500		1,500
	80 Buckingham at £70 per unit		5,600	5,600
equals	Contribution	1,000	2,400	3,400
less	Fixed overheads			2,000
equals	Profit			1,400

Summary:

The procedures for decision-making with limiting factors are:

- calculate the *contribution per unit of limiting factor* to make the decision as to which product to manufacture – the one with the higher contribution per unit of limiting factor will maximise profits

- calculate the profit statement using the *number of units of output* (and not the number of units of limiting factor)

- where there is a maximum level of output for the selected product, use as much of the limiting factor as possible, and then 'spill over' any unused limiting factor to the next best product (as in the Case Study)

Note that, where there are limiting factors, fewer of one or more products will be produced causing a shortfall in the market. It may be difficult to re-establish these products when full production can be resumed after the limiting factor has been resolved. The problem is that often customers want availability of all products and, if one isn't fully available, they won't buy the others (think of a store closing its carpet department and the effect on sales in the furniture department).

MARGINAL COSTING

In this chapter we have already applied the techniques of marginal costing to break-even analysis and the use of limiting factors.

Marginal cost is the cost of producing one extra unit of output.

Marginal cost is often – but not always – the total of the variable costs of producing a unit of output. For most purposes, marginal costing is not concerned with fixed costs (such as the rent of a factory); instead it is concerned with variable costs – direct materials, direct labour, direct expenses, and variable production overheads – which increase as output increases. For most decision-making, the marginal cost of a unit of output is, therefore, the variable cost of producing one more unit.

Knowing the marginal cost of a unit of output enables the management of a business or organisation to focus their attention on the *contribution* provided by each unit. As we have seen earlier, the contribution is the amount of money coming in from sales after marginal/variable costs have been paid. We usually express the calculation of contribution as:

selling price – variable cost = contribution

It can be calculated on a per unit basis, or for a batch of output (eg 1,000 units), or for a whole business or organisation.

The contribution, as its name implies, contributes to the cost of the overheads – once these are covered, the remainder of the contribution is profit. This has been seen already in break-even analysis where, after break-even point is reached, the contribution from additional sales adds to profit. Knowing the marginal cost of production helps with decision-making and, in the next section, we will see how it is used in making pricing decisions for 'special orders' and in the calculation of profit, and the valuation of closing stock.

Case Study

WYVERN BIKE COMPANY: MARGINAL COSTS

situation

The Wyvern Bike Company produces 100 bikes a week, and sells them for £200 each. Its costs are as follows:

weekly costs for producing 100 bikes	£
direct materials (£40 per bike)	4,000
direct labour (£50 per bike)	5,000
production overheads (fixed)	5,000
total cost	14,000

The factory has the capacity to produce 200 bikes a week, with no increase in production overheads.

As an accounts assistant at the Wyvern Bike Company, you are asked to:

- calculate the marginal cost of producing one bike
- calculate the contribution per bike
- prepare a weekly profit statement
- calculate the absorption cost of producing one bike
- give advice to the owner as to the price to be charged to a friend who wants a bike making next week – this will be extra to normal production and the owner wants to "cover the costs" but not make a profit

solution

- The marginal cost of producing one bike is:

	£
direct materials	40
direct labour	50
marginal cost per unit	90

The marginal cost is, here, the same as the variable cost (because production overheads are a fixed cost).

- The contribution per bike is:

$$\text{selling price} - \text{variable costs} = \text{contribution}$$
$$£200 \quad - \quad £90 \quad = £110$$

- The weekly profit statement for 100 bikes is:

		£	£
	sales (£200 per bike)		20,000
less	direct materials (£40 per bike)	4,000	
	direct labour (£50 per bike)	5,000	
			9,000
equals contribution			11,000
less	fixed costs (production overheads)		5,000
equals profit			6,000

- The absorption cost of producing one bike is:

	£
direct materials	40
direct labour	50
production overheads (£5,000 ÷ 100 bikes)	50
absorption cost per bike	140

- The friend will be charged £90, ie the variable cost, rather than the absorption cost of £140. (If you think the friend should pay £140, try reworking the profit statement, based on 101 bikes, and see if the owner has covered the costs or has made a profit.)

'SPECIAL ORDER' PRICING

'Special order' pricing is where a business uses spare capacity to make extra sales of its product at a lower price than its normal selling price. Such pricing is normally used once the business is profitable at its current level of output, ie it has reached break-even. Additional sales – at 'special order' prices – can be made at a selling price above marginal cost, but below absorption cost. In this way, profits can be increased, provided that the additional sales are spare capacity. The key to increasing profit from additional sales is to ensure that a contribution to profit is made from the special order: the Case Study (below) illustrates this principle.

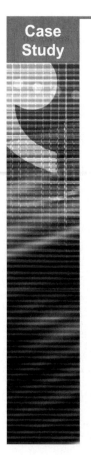

Case Study

WYVERN BIKE COMPANY: SPECIAL ORDERS

situation

The Wyvern Bike Company produces 100 bikes a week, and sells them for £200 each. Its costs are as follows:

weekly costs for producing 100 bikes

	£
direct materials (£40 per bike)	4,000
direct labour (£50 per bike)	5,000
production overheads (fixed)	5,000
total cost	14,000

The owner of the company has been approached by a mail order warehouse which wishes to buy:

- *either* 50 bikes each week at a price of £120 per bike
- *or* 100 bikes each week at a price of £80 per bike

The bikes can be produced in addition to existing production, with no increase in overheads. The special order is not expected to affect the company's existing sales. How would you advise the owner?

solution

The *absorption cost* of producing one bike is £140 (£14,000 ÷ 100 bikes). The mail order warehouse is offering either £120 or £80 per bike. On the face of it, with an absorption cost of £140, both orders should be rejected. However, as there will be no increase in production overheads, we can use *marginal costing* to help with decision-making.

The *marginal cost* per bike is £90 (direct materials £40 + direct labour £50), and so any contribution, ie selling price less marginal cost, will be profit:

- **50 bikes at £120 each**

  Although below absorption cost, the offer price of £120 is above the marginal cost of £90 and increases profit by the amount of the £30 extra contribution, ie (£120 – £90) x 50 bikes = £1,500 extra profit.

- **100 bikes at £80 each**

  This offer price is below absorption cost of £140 and marginal cost of £90; therefore there will be a fall in profit if this order is undertaken of (£80 – £90) x 100 bikes = £1,000 reduced profit.

weekly profit statements

	Existing production of 100 units	Existing production + 50 units @ £120 each	Existing production + 100 units @ £80 each
	£	£	£
Sales revenue (per week):			
100 bikes at £200 each	20,000	20,000	20,000
50 bikes at £120 each	–	6,000	–
100 bikes at £80 each	–	–	8,000
	20,000	26,000	28,000
Less production costs:			
Direct materials (£40 per unit)	4,000	6,000	8,000
Direct labour (£50 per unit)	5,000	7,500	10,000
Production overheads (fixed)	5,000	5,000	5,000
PROFIT	6,000	7,500	5,000

The conclusion is that the first special order from the mail order warehouse should be accepted, and the second declined. The general rule is that, once the fixed overheads have been recovered (ie break-even has been reached), provided additional units can be sold at a price above marginal cost, then profits will increase.

COST AND REVENUE PLANNING

The techniques of marginal costing can also be used to establish the effect of changes in costs and revenues on the profit of the business. Such changes include

– a reduction in selling prices in order to sell a greater number of units of output and to increase profits

– an increase in selling prices (which may cause a reduction in the number of units sold) in order to increase profits

Any change in selling prices and output will have an effect on revenues and the variable costs; there may also be an effect on fixed costs. The best way to show such changes is to use a columnar layout which shows costs and revenues as they are at present and then – in further columns – how they will be affected by any proposed changes. This method is used in the Case Study which follows.

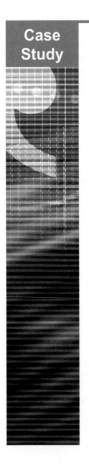

Case Study

BROOKES AND COMPANY:
COST AND REVENUE PLANNING

situation

Brookes and Company produces tool kits for bikes. The company produces 100,000 tool kits each year and the costs per unit of output are:

	£
	£
direct materials	2.20
direct labour	2.00
variable production overheads	0.80
fixed production overheads	0.40
fixed non-production overheads	0.60
	6.00

The selling price per tool kit is £10.00

The managing director of the business, John Brookes, has been thinking about how to increase profits for next year. He has asked you, as an accounts assistant, to look at the following two proposals from a cost accounting viewpoint.

Proposal 1

To reduce the selling price of each tool kit to £9.00. This is expected to increase sales by 20,000 kits each year to a total of 120,000 kits. Apart from changes in variable costs, there would be no change in fixed costs.

Proposal 2

To increase the selling price of each tool kit to £12.00. This is expected to reduce sales by 20,000 kits each year to a total of 80,000 kits. Apart from changes in variable costs, there would be a reduction of £5,000 in fixed production overheads.

You are to write a memorandum to John Brookes stating your advice, giving reasons and workings. Each of the two proposals is to be considered on its own merits without reference to the other proposal.

solution

The following calculations, presented in columnar format, will form an appendix to the memorandum to John Brookes. Note that the three money columns deal with the existing production level, and then the two proposals.

BROOKES AND COMPANY

Cost and revenue planning for next year

	existing output (100,000 units) £	proposal 1 (120,000 units) £	proposal 2 (80,000 units) £
Sales:			
100,000 units at £10.00 per unit	1,000,000		
120,000 units at £9.00 per unit		1,080,000	
80,000 units at £12.00 per unit			960,000
TOTAL REVENUE	1,000,000	1,080,000	960,000
Direct materials at £2.20 per unit	220,000	264,000	176,000
Direct labour at £2.00 per unit	200,000	240,000	160,000
Variable production overhead at £0.80 per unit	80,000	96,000	64,000
Fixed production overhead	40,000	40,000	35,000
Fixed non-production overhead	60,000	60,000	60,000
TOTAL COSTS	600,000	700,000	495,000
PROFIT	400,000	380,000	465,000

Tutorial notes:
- fixed production overheads: 100,000 units at £0.40 per unit (note £5,000 reduction under proposal 2)
- fixed non-production overheads: 100,000 units at £0.60 per unit

MEMORANDUM

To:	Managing Director
From:	Accounts Assistant
Date:	Today

Cost and revenue plans for next year

Introduction

- You asked for my comments on the proposals for next year's production.

- I have looked at the expected profits if

    - we continue to sell 100,000 units each year at a selling price of £10.00 each

    - selling price is reduced to £9.00 per unit, with sales volume expected to increase to 120,000 units each year

    - selling price is increased to £12.00 per unit, with sales volume expected to decrease to 80,000 units each year

Report

- Please refer to the calculations sheet.

- At existing levels of production, the contribution (selling price – variable costs) per unit is:

    £10.00 – (£2.20 + £2.00 + £0.80) = £5.00 per unit x 100,000 units = £500,000

    Fixed costs total £100,000.

    Therefore profit is £400,000.

- For proposal 1, the contribution per unit is:

    £9.00 – (£2.20 + £2.00 + £0.80) = £4.00 per unit x 120,000 units = £480,000

    Fixed costs total £100,000

    Therefore profit is £380,000.

- For proposal 2, the contribution per unit is:

    £12.00 – (£2.20 + £2.00 + £0.80) = £7.00 per unit x 80,000 units = £560,000

    Fixed costs total £95,000.

    Therefore profit is £465,000.

Conclusion

- Proposal 2 maximises the contribution from each unit of output.

- Although we expect to sell fewer units, the total contribution is greater.

- There is a small reduction in fixed costs under this proposal.

- Before proposal 2 is adopted, we would need to be sure of the accuracy of the expected fall in sales volume.

MARGINAL COSTING: OTHER POINTS

We have seen how marginal costing techniques can be useful in decision-making. Nevertheless, there are a number of points that must be borne in mind:

- *fixed costs must be covered*

  A balance needs to be struck between the output that is sold at above marginal cost and the output that is sold at absorption cost. The overall contribution from output must cover the fixed costs of the business and provide a profit. Overall output should be sold at a high enough price to provide a contribution to fixed costs.

- *separate markets for marginal cost*

  It is sensible business practice to separate out the markets where marginal cost is used. For example, a business would not quote a price based on absorption cost to retailer A and a price based on marginal cost to retailer B, when A and B are both in the same town! It would be better to seek new markets – perhaps abroad – with prices based on marginal cost.

- *effect on customers*

  One of the problems of using marginal cost pricing to attract new business is that it is difficult to persuade the customer to pay closer to, or above, absorption cost later on. Thus one of the dangers of using marginal cost is that profits can be squeezed quite dramatically if the technique is used too widely.

- *problems of product launch on marginal cost basis*

  There is great temptation to launch a new product at the keenest possible price – below absorption cost (but above marginal cost). If the product is highly successful, it could well alter the cost structure of the business. However, it could also lead to the collapse of sales of older products so that most sales are derived from output priced on the marginal cost basis – it may then be difficult to increase up prices to above absorption cost levels.

- *special edition products*

  Many businesses use marginal costing techniques to sell off older products at a keen price. For example, car manufacturers with a new model due in a few months' time will package the old model with 'special edition' bodywork and sell it at a low price (but above marginal cost).

MARGINAL COSTING AND ABSORPTION COSTING

In this chapter we have used marginal costing techniques in short-term decision-making. Nevertheless, we must always remember that one of the objectives of the costing system is to ensure that all the costs of a business or organisation are recovered by being charged to production. This is achieved by means of absorption costing (see Chapter 5). We will now make a comparison between the two methods of costing.

- *marginal costing*

    As we have seen in this chapter, the technique of marginal costing recognises that fixed costs vary with time rather than activity, and attempts to identify the cost of producing one extra unit. For example, the rent of a factory relates to a certain time period, eg one month, and remains unchanged whether 100 units of output are made or whether 500 units are made (always assuming that the capacity of the factory is at least 500 units); by contrast, the production of one extra unit will incur an increase in variable costs, ie direct materials, direct labour and direct expenses (if any) – this increase is the *marginal cost*.

- *absorption costing*

    This technique absorbs all production costs into each unit of output (see Chapter 5). Thus each unit of output in a factory making 100 units will bear a greater proportion of the factory rent than will each unit when 500 units are made in the same time period.

The diagram below demonstrates how the terms in marginal costing relate to the same production costs as those categorised under absorption costing terms. As noted above, when using marginal costing it is the behaviour of the cost – fixed or variable – that is important, not the origin of the cost.

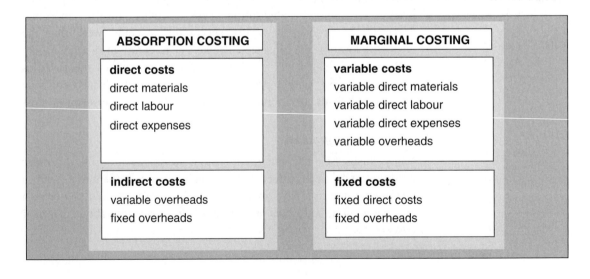

marginal costing and absorption costing: profit comparisons

Because of the different ways in which marginal costing and absorption costing treat fixed costs, the two techniques produce different levels of profit when there is a closing stock figure. This is because, under marginal costing, the closing stock is valued at variable production cost; by contrast, absorption cost includes a share of fixed production costs in the closing stock valuation. This is illustrated in the Case Study which follows, looking at the effect of using marginal costing and absorption costing on the profit statement of a manufacturing business.

Note that the marginal cost approach is used to help with the decision-making process – as we have seen in this chapter with break-even, limiting factors, 'special order' pricing, and cost and revenue planning. However, for financial accounting, absorption costing must be used for stock valuation purposes in order to comply with SSAP 9 (see page 58). Under SSAP 9, the closing stock valuation is based on the costs of direct materials, direct labour, direct expenses (if any), and production overheads. Note that non-production overheads are not included, as they are charged in full to the profit statement in the year to which they relate.

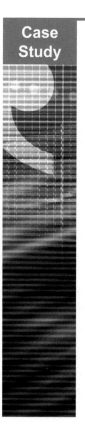

Case Study

CHAIRS LIMITED: MARGINAL AND ABSORPTION COSTING

situation

Chairs Limited commenced business on 1 January 2007. It manufactures a special type of chair designed to alleviate back pain. Information on the first year's trading is as follows:

number of chairs manufactured	5,000
number of chairs sold	4,500
selling price	£110 per chair
direct materials	£30 per chair
direct labour	£40 per chair
fixed production overheads	£100,000

The directors ask for your help in producing profit statements using the marginal costing and absorption costing techniques. They say that they will use 'the one that shows the higher profit' to the company's bank manager.

solution

CHAIRS LIMITED

Profit statement for the year ended 31 December 2007

	MARGINAL COSTING		ABSORPTION COSTING	
	£	£	£	£
Sales at £110 each		495,000		495,000
Variable costs				
Direct materials at £30 each	150,000		150,000	
Direct labour at £40 each	200,000		200,000	
	350,000			
Less Closing stock (marginal cost)				
500 chairs at £70 each	35,000			
	315,000			
Fixed production overheads	100,000		100,000	
			450,000	
Less Closing stock (absorption cost)				
500 chairs at £90 each			45,000	
Less Cost of goods sold		415,000		405,000
PROFIT		80,000		90,000

Tutorial notes:

- Closing stock is always calculated on the basis of this year's costs:

  marginal costing, variable costs only, ie £30 + £40 = £70 per chair

  absorption costing, variable and fixed costs, ie £450,000 ÷ 5,000 chairs = £90 per chair

- The difference in the profit figures is caused only by the closing stock figures: £35,000 under marginal costing and £45,000 under absorption costing – the same costs have been used, but fixed production overheads have been treated differently.

- Only fixed production overheads are dealt with differently using the techniques of marginal and absorption costing – both methods charge non-production overheads *in full* to the profit statement in the year to which they relate.

With marginal costing, the full amount of the fixed production overheads has been charged in this year's profit statement; by contrast, with absorption costing, part of the fixed production overheads (here, £10,000) has been carried forward in the stock valuation.

- Project A has a lower NPV than Project B – this is because of a lower initial cost. This imbalance of initial cost is neutralised by the IRR calculation, which shows Project A to be superior.

- On balance, Project A is recommended:
  - lower initial cost
  - high cash inflows in the first two years
  - quick payback
  - positive NPV
  - higher IRR in relation to the company's required rate of return

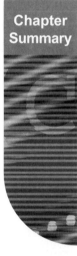

Chapter Summary

- Capital investment appraisal uses a number of methods to help in management decision-making.
- The main methods are payback period and discounted cash flow.
- Businesses often use a combination of appraisal methods before making long-term decisions about major projects.
- Internal rate of return (also known as DCF yield) is used to rank projects, while still applying the principles of discounted cash flow.
- Before authorising a capital project, other considerations include:
  - total implications for the organisation
  - cost of finance, and effect of changes
  - taxation
  - forecasting techniques to answer 'what if?' questions

Key Terms

capital investment appraisal	enables a business or organisation to make long-term decisions whether or not to invest in a particular capital investment project and, where there are alternatives, to help to decide in which to invest
cost of capital	The percentage cost of financing an investment – either the rate of return that the business expects on its money, or the rate of interest it has to pay when borrowing
payback period	time period for the initial outlay to be repaid by the net cash inflow
discounted cash flow	capital investment appraisal technique that uses cash flows and recognises the time value of money

net present value (NPV)	the value of cash outflows and inflows for a project discounted to present-day amounts
internal rate of return (IRR)	the rate of return at which the net present value of cash inflows equals the cost of the initial investment

Student Activities

TABLE OF DISCOUNTED CASH FLOW FACTORS

Cost of capital/ rate of return	10%	12%	14%	16%	18%	20%	22%	24%
Year 1	0.909	0.893	0.877	0.862	0.847	0.833	0.820	0.806
Year 2	0.826	0.797	0.769	0.743	0.718	0.694	0.672	0.650
Year 3	0.751	0.712	0.675	0.641	0.609	0.579	0.551	0.524
Year 4	0.683	0.636	0.592	0.552	0.516	0.482	0.451	0.423
Year 5	0.621	0.567	0.519	0.476	0.437	0.402	0.370	0.341
Year 6	0.564	0.507	0.456	0.410	0.370	0.335	0.303	0.275

Tutorial note: In Examinations you will always be given the appropriate factors.

9.1 Robert Smith is considering two major capital investment projects for his business. Only one project can be chosen and the following information is available:

	Project Exe	Project Wye
	£	£
Initial cost at the beginning of the project	80,000	100,000
Net cash inflows, year: 1	40,000	20,000
2	40,000	30,000
3	20,000	50,000
4	10,000	50,000
5	10,000	40,000

The initial cost occurs at the beginning of the project and you may assume that the net cash inflows will arise at the end of each year. Smith requires an annual rate of return of 12 per cent. Neither project will have any residual value at the end of five years.

To help Robert Smith make his decision, as accounts assistant you are to:

- produce numerical assessments of the two projects based on the following capital investment appraisal methods:

  (a)   the payback period

  (b)   the net present value

- write a report to Robert Smith on the relative merits of the project appraisal methods, and advise him which capital investment, if either, should be undertaken.

9.2   Sesame Shoes Limited manufactures shoes at its factory in Wyvern. The company requires an annual rate of return of 10% on any new project. The Managing Director has asked you to appraise the financial effects of developing a new range of shoes. You are given the following information relating to this project.

| | Year 0 | Year 1 | Year 2 | Year 3 | Year 4 | Year 5 |
	£000	£000	£000	£000	£000	£000
Design costs	–	95	–	–	–	–
Sales revenue	–	–	60	80	100	50
Variable costs	–	–	30	40	50	25
10% Present value factor	1.000	0.909	0.826	0.751	0.683	0.621

Task 1

Calculate for the new project:

(a)   the payback period

(b)   the net present value

Task 2

A few days after submitting your calculations to the Managing Director, she says to you:

"I have calculated the internal rate of return on the new project to be almost 20 per cent. What I don't understand is whether this is good or bad in relation to the 10 per cent return we require on new projects."

Explain the significance of the internal rate of return in relation to the return required on new projects. (There is no need to show how IRR is calculated.)

9.3 You are an accounts assistant at Durning Foods Limited. The company produces ready meals which are sold in supermarkets and convenience stores. You have just received the following memorandum from the general manager:

MEMORANDUM

To: Accounts Assistant

From: General Manager

Date: 10 November 2007

Purchase of delivery vehicles

We are considering the purchase and operation of our own fleet of delivery vehicles at the end of this year.

The distribution manager tells me that we will be able to cancel our current delivery contract and, as a result, there will be cash savings of £28,300 each year from 2008 onwards, after taking account of the vehicle operating costs.

The vehicles will cost us £80,000 and will have a resale value of £10,000 when they are sold at the end of 2011.

Please appraise this proposal from a financial viewpoint. I need to know the payback period and the net present value. As you know, the maximum required payback period is three years and, for net present value, we require a return of 12 per cent.

Task 1

Use the working paper on the next page to calculate the net present value and the payback period of the proposed investment. Ignore inflation and calculate all money amounts to the nearest £.

Task 2

Write a report, dated 12 November 2007, to the General Manager evaluating the proposal from a financial viewpoint. State any assumptions you have made in your analysis. (Use a copy of the report form in the Appendix.)

DURNING FOODS LIMITED

Working paper for the financial appraisal of purchase of delivery vehicles

DISCOUNTED CASH FLOW

Year	Cash Flow	Discount Factor at 12%	Discounted Cash Flow
	£		£
2007	_____	1.000	_____
2008	_____	0.893	_____
2009	_____	0.797	_____
2010	_____	0.712	_____
2011	_____	0.636	_____
Net Present Value (NPV)			▬▬▬▬▬

PAYBACK PERIOD

Year	Cash Flow	Cumulative Cash Flow
	£	£
2007	_____	_____
2008	_____	_____
2009	_____	_____
2010	_____	_____
2011	_____	_____

Payback period = _____

9.4 The Wyvern Bike Company is planning to introduce a new range of bikes in addition to its existing range. The company requires an annual rate of return of 12 per cent on any new project. The Managing Director has asked you, the accounts assistant, to appraise the financial effects of introducing the new range. You are given the following information relating to this project (see next page).

	Year 0 £000	Year 1 £000	Year 2 £000	Year 3 £000	Year 4 £000	Year 5 £000
Development costs	40	60	–	–	–	–
Sales revenue	–	–	75	90	150	100
Variable costs	–	–	30	36	60	40
12% Present value factor	1.000	0.893	0.797	0.712	0.636	0.567

Task 1

Calculate for the new project:

(a) the payback period

(b) the net present value

Task 2

Use the data from Task 1 to prepare a report to the Managing Director on the new bike project. Your report should be based on the format shown in this chapter and will:

(a) identify *two* additional items of information relevant to appraising this project

(b) make a recommendation to accept or reject the project based on its net present value

9.5 Ken Jones needs some equipment for his printing firm. He has to choose between the following methods of acquisition:

• purchase of the equipment for cash

• purchase under a hire purchase contract, involving an initial deposit and two annual payments

• leasing the equipment

The following information is available:

– cash price of equipment	£10,000
– period of use in Jones' firm	5 years
– scrap value at end of use	£1,000
– initial deposit under hire purchase contract	£4,000
– two annual hire purchase payments due at end of first year and end of second year	£4,000 each
– leasing equipment, five annual hire charge payments due at end of each year	£2,500 each

Ken Jones requires a rate of return over the five year period of 10 per cent per annum.

To assist Ken Jones make his decision, you are asked to:

• produce numerical appraisals of the three methods of acquisition using the net present value method

• advise Ken Jones of the best method of acquisition

Answers to student activities

CHAPTER 1: AN INTRODUCTION TO COST ACCOUNTING

1.1 (a) • The principle behind this Student Activity is the identification of relevant costs
   • Whilst the type of organisation selected may well not fit with the exact layout for a manufacturing business, as shown on page 17, the Activity should generate thought and discussion of costs involved
   • As an example, an outline of the costs incurred by a school or college is as follows:

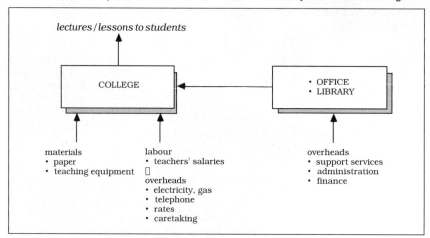

(b) • What are the units of output of the organisation to which costs can be charged?
   • The main sections of the organisation should be identified. Does the costing system in use charge costs to these sections, whether or not they are formally called cost centres?
   • In the school/college described above, the example cost unit is student hours, and cost centres examples are teaching departments, learning resources, administration.

1.2 Suggestions to include:

	COST UNIT	COST CENTRE
college of further education	student hour	teaching department learning resources administration
mixed farm	kilo of wheat head of cattle	field cattle shed

1.3 (a) See text, pages 21 and 22
   (b) • raw materials: variable
   • factory rent: fixed
   • telephone: semi-variable
   • direct labour: variable
   • indirect labour: fixed
   • commission to sales staff: variable

Classifying costs by nature identifies them as being fixed, or semi-variable, or variable. This helps with decision making – the business might be able to alter the balance between fixed and variable costs in order to increase profits.For example, a furniture manufacturing business will have to make decisions on whether to use direct labour (variable cost) or machinery (fixed cost) for many of the production processes. The decision will be based very much on the expected level of sales, ie for lower sales it is likely to make greater use of direct labour, while for higher sales a more machine-intensive method of production might be used.

1.4

tubular steel	direct materials
factory supervisor's salary	indirect labour
wages of employee operating moulding machine	direct labour
works canteen assistant's wages	indirect labour
rates of factory	indirect expenses
power to operate machines	indirect expenses*
factory heating and lighting	indirect expenses
plastic for making chair seats	direct materials
hire of special machinery for one particular order	direct expenses
cost of grease for the moulding machine	indirect materials
depreciation of factory machinery	indirect expenses
depreciation of office equipment	indirect expenses

*   Note: the cost of power to operate machines has been classified above as an indirect expense. This is often the case because it is not worthwhile analysing the cost of power for each unit of production. An industry that uses a lot of power will often have meters fitted to each machine so that costs may be identified and allocated to production as a direct expense. Other, lesser users of power, are unlikely to calculate the separate cost and will consider power to be an indirect expense. Whichever treatment is used, it is important that it is applied consistently.

1.5

COST ITEM	CLASSIFICATION (write your answer)
Dressings	direct materials
Disposable scalpels	direct materials
Surgeon's salary	direct labour
Floor cleaning materials	indirect materials
Laundry	indirect expenses*
Depreciation of staff drinks machine	indirect expenses*
Theatre heat and light	indirect expenses*
Porter's wages	indirect labour
Anaesthetic gas	direct materials
Depreciation of theatre equipment	indirect expenses
Maintenance of theatre equipment	indirect expenses
Cost of CDs for music in theatre	indirect expenses
Anaesthetist's salary	direct labour

*   These items have been classified as indirect expenses – this is the most likely classification. If the money amount of any item was large, it would be worthwhile looking at the costing system to see if the item could be identified as a direct expense.

1.6

Cost item	Total cost £	Prime cost £	Production overheads £	Admin costs £	Selling and distribution costs £
Wages of employees working on the bottling line	6,025	6,025			
Wages of employees in the stores department	2,750		2,750		
Cost of bottles	4,050	4,050			
Safety goggles for bottling line employees	240		240		
Advertisement for new employees	125			125	
Depreciation of bottling machinery	500		500		
Depreciation of sales staff's cars	1,000				1,000
Royalty paid to local farmer	750	750			
Cost of trade exhibition	1,500				1,500
Computer stationery	210			210	
Sales staff salaries	4,095				4,095
TOTALS	21,245	10,825	3,490	335	6,595

1.7 (a)

Hughes Limited
Total cost statement for the year ended 31 December 2007

	£	£
Direct materials		118,830
Direct labour		117,315
PRIME COST		236,145
Production overheads		
rent and rates	16,460	
factory power	3,825	
factory heat and light	1,185	
factory expenses and maintenance	4,095	
depreciation of factory plant and machinery	3,725	
		29,290
PRODUCTION COST		265,435

Non-production overheads

Selling and distribution costs:

advertising	11,085

Administration costs:

office salaries and wages	69,350	
office expenses	3,930	
		73,280
TOTAL COST		349,800

Note: It has been assumed in the cost statement that:

- all of the raw materials used in the factory are direct materials
- all of the factory wages are direct labour − with additional information, it would be possible to split the cost between direct and indirect labour

(b)

Hughes Limited
Profit statement for the year ended 31 December 2007

		£
	Sales	426,350
less	Total cost	349,800
	PROFIT	76,550

CHAPTER 2: MATERIALS COSTS

2.1   *Stock item D*

- maximum space = 350 units; maximum usage = 95 days x 3 units per day = 285 units; therefore maximum stock is 285 units
- minimum stock = 10 days x 3 units per day = 30 units
- re-order level = 30 units + (7 days x 3 units per day) = 51 units
- re-order quantity = 285 units − 30 units = 255 units

Stock item E

- maximum space = 350 units; maximum usage = 95 days x 4 units per day = 380; therefore maximum stock is 350 units
- minimum stock = 10 days x 4 units per day = 40 units
- re-order level = 40 units + (7 days x 4 units per day) = 68 units
- re-order quantity = 350 units − 40 units = 310 units

2.2

STOCK RECORD

Stock Description	A4 yellow card		
Stock units	reams	Minimum	36 reams
Stock Ref. No.	A4/Y3	Maximum	105 reams
Location	row7, bin5	Re-order level	66 reams
		Re-order quantity	69 reams

DATE	GOODS RECEIVED		GOODS ISSUED		BALANCE
	Reference	Quantity	Reference	Quantity	
2007					
1 May					84
4 May			MR184	18	66
6 May			MR187	20	46
10 May			MR188	10	36
14 May	GRN4507	69			105
17 May			MR394	20	85
20 May			MR401	11	74
26 May			MR422	6	68

2.3 (a)   stock record

    (b)   stock list

    (c)   stock reconciliation

    (d)   cost and net realisable value

AVCO

STORES LEDGER RECORD: TYPE Y

Date	Receipts			Issues			Balance		
2007	Quantity	Cost	Total Cost	Quantity	Cost	Total Cost	Quantity	Cost	Total Cost
		£	£		£	£		£	£
January	200	10.00	2,000.00				200	10.00	2,000.00
February	100	9.50	950.00				200	10.00	2,000.00
							100	9.50	950.00
							300	9.83	2,950.00
March				240	9.83	2,360.00	60	9.83	590.00
April	100	10.50	1,050.00				60	9.83	590.00
							100	10.50	1,050.00
							160	10.25	1,640.00
May	140	10.00	1,400.00				160	10.25	1,640.00
							140	10.00	1,400.00
							300	10.13	3,040.00
June				100	10.13	1,013.00	200	10.13	2,027.00

Note: some figures have been rounded to the nearest penny

Balance sheet valuation at 30 June 2007:

	£	
Type X	824.00	(cost price, using FIFO)
Type Y	1,950.00	(net realisable value)
	2,774.00	

2.6 Task 1

STORES LEDGER RECORD

Product: Wholewheat flour

Date 2007	Receipts			Issues			Balance	
	Quantity kgs	Cost per kg £	Total Cost £	Quantity kgs	Cost per kg £	Total Cost £	Quantity kgs	Total Cost £
Balance at 1 May							10,000	2,500
6 May	20,000	0.30	6,000				30,000	8,500
10 May				20,000	10,000 x 0.25	2,500	10,000	3,000
					10,000 x 0.30	3,000		
						5,500		
17 May	10,000	0.35	3,500				10,000	3,000
							10,000	3,500
20 May				15,000	10,000 x 0.30	3,000	5,000	1,750
					5,000 x 0.35	1,750		
						4,750		

Task 2

2007	Code	Debit	Credit
6 May	3000	£6,000	
6 May	5000		£6,000
10 May	3000		£5,500*
10 May	3300	£5,500	
17 May	3000	£3,500	
17 May	5000		£3,500
20 May	3000		£4,750**
20 May	3300	£4,750	

* £2,500 + £3,000   ** £3,000 + £1,750

CHAPTER 3: LABOUR COSTS

3.1   N Ball: 35 hours x £8.00 per hour = £280.00 (no bonus)

T Smith: 37 hours x £9.00 per hour = £333.00 + bonus £9.00 = £342.00

L Lewis: 40 hours x £10.00 per hour = £400.00 + bonus £13.75 = £413.75

M Wilson: 38 hours x £7.00 per hour = £266.00 + bonus £4.08 = £270.08

3.2

MEMORANDUM	
To:	Office Manager
From:	Accounts Assistant
Date:	Today

Remuneration of production-line workers

I have been asked to produce a report on remuneration methods for production-line workers.

At present the company pays these workers on a time-rate basis. The main advantages of such a system from the viewpoint of both employer and employees are as follows:

- it is easy to calculate and understand
- there is no requirement to establish time allowances and piecework rates
- employees receive a regular wage, which is unaffected by fluctuations in output
- the system can be applied to all direct labour employees
- the quality of finished output does not suffer as a result of hurried work

The disadvantages of time rate are that:

- all production-line employees are paid the same, whether they work efficiently or inefficiently
- no incentive is given to employees to work harder
- the company needs to employ supervisors to ensure that output is maintained
- slow working by employees does not affect the basic wage, but could lead to the company having to pay overtime rates to ensure that output is completed.

Employee representatives have approached the company management with a request that other remuneration methods be considered. In particular piecework systems, or a time rate with a production bonus system have been suggested.

A *piecework system* is where payment is based on the quantity of output.

The main advantages of this are that:

- payment of wages is linked directly to output
- more efficient workers earn more than those who are less efficient
- work is done quicker and less time is wasted

The main disadvantages are that:

- the system is not suitable for all direct labour employees
- there may be difficulty in agreeing piecework rates between employer and employees

- the quality of the finished product may be low and more inspectors may be needed
- control system will be needed to check the amount produced by each worker
- from the employer's point of view, the quality of the finished product may be low
- pay calculations will be more complex

Employees need to be aware that pay is reduced if there are production problems, eg machine breakdown, or shortage of materials. A way around this is to use a piecework system with a guaranteed time rate. A further disadvantage is that there may be difficulties in agreeing piecework rates.

A time rate with a production bonus is a system used to encourage employees to be more efficient where work is not so repetitive. There are a number of variations of bonus including increased bonuses for higher levels of output, and group bonuses paid to groups of employees.

The main advantages of bonus systems are that:

- wages are linked to output, but a minimum wage – the time rate – is guaranteed each week
- work is done quicker and less time is wasted
- the more efficient workers earn more
- a bonus system can often be applied to the entire workforce

The disadvantages are that:

- from the employee's point of view, the bonus is not paid if circumstances such as machine breakdown, or shortage of materials occur
- from the employer's point of view, the quality of the finished product may be low and more inspectors will be needed
- there may be difficulty in agreeing bonus rates with employees
- control procedures are needed, and pay calculations will be more complex

Conclusion

Each of the three main methods of remuneration has advantages and disadvantages. In selecting a suitable system both employer and employee must consider that:

- reward should be related to effort and fair to all staff
- the system should be easy to manage and administer, and be cheap and efficient to run
- it should be easy for employees to understand how pay is calculated
- payment should be made at regular intervals and soon after the event
- the principles of the scheme should remain constant, but there should be flexibility to deal with changes in production techniques

3.3 (a) • L Fry: £400.00 (time rate)
  • R Williams: £315.00 (piecework rate)
  • P Grant: £362.50 (piecework rate)

(b) • not suitable for all direct labour employees
  • employees' pay is reduced if there are production problems
  • quality of the finished product may be low
  • more inspectors may be needed

- control systems needed to check the amount produced by each worker
- more complex pay calculations
- may be difficulty in agreeing piecework rates with employees

3.4   Gross wages

		£
• Steve Kurtin:	35 hours at £5.50 per hour =	192.50
	4 hours overtime at £7.333 per hour =	29.33
	production bonus 45 x 25p =	11.25
		233.08
• Pete Singh:	35 hours at £6.50 per hour =	227.50
	3 hours overtime at £8.667 per hour =	26.00
	4 hours overtime at £9.75 per hour =	39.00
	production bonus 57 x 25p =	14.25
		306.75

Piecework rate for Steve Kurtin
£233.08 ÷ 45 = £5.18 per 1,000 copies printed

3.5

	MOULDING	FINISHING
• Standard hours saved	–	500
• Bonus (£)	–	2,025*
• Total labour cost (£)	31,160	38,475

*   £36,450 ÷ 4,500 hours = £8.10 x 500 hours = £4,050 ÷ 2 = £2,025

3.6   (a) Week 1: 400 hours at £6.20 per hour = £2,480

50 hours at 1.5 x £6.20 = 50 x £9.30 = £465

Total gross earnings for Week1 = £2,480 + £465 = £2,945

Week 2: 400 hours at £6.20 per hour = £2,480 = Total gross earnings

(b) Week 1: Normally treated as indirect labour cost would be overtime premium on 50 hours, ie 50 x 0.5 x £6.20 = £155

Week 2: Normally treated as indirect labour cost would be 20 hours of non-production work at basic pay, ie 20 x £6.20 = £124

3.7   • *work-in-progress £2,100:* the cost of direct labour incurred by the company for the work on manufacturing the product

- *production overheads £900:* the cost of indirect labour incurred by the company for the week
- *non-production overheads £700:* the administration labour costs for the week
- *total payroll for the week £3,700:* the total of net wages paid to employees, income tax and National Insurance Contributions, and pension contributions

3.8   Task 1

Dr		Wages Control Account		Cr
	£			£
Cash/bank (net wages)	7,500	Work-in-progress (direct labour)		6,500
HMRC (income tax and NIC)	1,450	Production overheads		
Pension contributions	750	(indirect labour)		2,700
		Non-production overheads		
		(administration)		500
	9,700			9,700

Task 2

2007	Code	Debit	Credit
26 March	3300	£6,500	
26 March	5200		£6,500
26 March	3500	£2,700	
26 March	5200		£2,700
26 March	3700	£500	
26 March	5200		£500

3.9   Total cost of direct labour for October:

			£
14,400 hours	x £8 per hour	=	115,200
1,600 hours	x £12 (£8 + £4) per hour	=	19,200
16,000 hours			134,400

Cost book-keeping entries:

	Debit	Credit
	£	£
• work-in-progress – 'Mulligan' clubs (1500)	134,400	
• wages control (5000)		134,400

CHAPTER 4: EXPENSES

4.1   (a)   *Capital expenditure:* expenditure incurred on the purchase, alteration or improvement of fixed assets. Examples: purchase of premises, vehicles, machinery; legal costs of buying property; installation and setting up of a machine.

(b)   *Revenue expenditure:* expenditure incurred on running costs. Examples: fuel for vehicles; repairs to premises; labour costs of running the business.

4.2 (a) *Direct expenses:* those expenses that are attributable to particular units of output. Examples: royalties payable to the designer of a product; special items bought in for a particular product or job; power costs metered to output; depreciation methods linked directly to output (such as units of output or service method).

(b) *Indirect expenses:* those expenses that are not attributable directly to particular units of output. Examples: rent and rates, heating and lighting, depreciation methods not linked directly to output (such as straight-line and reducing balance methods).

4.3 Fred Jarvis' wages will be shown in wages control account as:

    – *debit* cash/bank, income tax and NIC, and pension contributions

    – *credit* property account

Thus the cost of his labour is debited to the fixed asset account of property (rather than work-in-progress, as would be the usual case for production-line employees). As he is building an extension to the warehouse, his wages (and also the cost of the materials he uses) are treated as capital expenditure because he is adding to the value of a fixed asset.

4.4 **Graph A**

- shows a *fixed cost,* which remains constant over a range of output levels
- as output increases, the *cost per unit* falls
- at an output beyond the limit of the graph, the fixed cost will increase as another factory needs to be rented; the nature of such a cost is known as a *stepped fixed cost.*

Graph B

- shows a *variable cost,* which alters directly with changes in output levels
- as output increases then the cost increases, ie the cost per unit remains the same

4.5

		capital expenditure	revenue expenditure
(a)	purchase of motor vehicles	✓	
(b)	depreciation of motor vehicles		✓
(c)	payment of office rent		✓
(d)	salaries of office staff		✓
(e)	legal fees relating to the purchase of property	✓	
(f)	re-decoration of office		✓
(g)	installation of air-conditioning in office	✓	
(h)	wages of own employees used to build extension to the stockroom	✓	
(i)	installation and setting up of a new machine	✓	

4.6

		direct expenses	indirect expenses	either*
(a)	hire of machinery for a particular job	✓		
(b)	office rent		✓	
(c)	cleaning materials		✓	
(d)	power costs			✓
(e)	royalty paid to designer for each unit of output	✓		
(f)	sales staff car expenses		✓	
(g)	depreciation of production machinery			✓
(h)	consultant's fees relating to a particular job	✓		
(i)	heating and lighting		✓	

(d) Power costs are direct expenses where machinery is separately metered and used for a particular product or job; otherwise, they are indirect expenses.

(g) Depreciation of production machinery is a direct expense when the depreciation method is linked directly to output (such as units of output or service method; it is an indirect expense when the depreciation method is not linked directly to output (such as straight-line and reducing balance methods).

4.7

		fixed	semi-fixed	variable
(a)	rates of business premises	✓		
(b)	royalty paid to designer for each unit of output			✓
(c)	car hire with fixed rental and charge per mile		✓	
(d)	employees paid on piecework basis			✓
(e)	straight-line depreciation	✓		
(f)	units of output depreciation			✓
(g)	direct materials			✓
(h)	telephone bill with fixed rental and charge per unit		✓	
(i)	office salaries	✓		

4.8 (a) cleaning materials for the machines: indirect materials
(b) wages of factory supervisor: indirect labour
(c) clay from which pots are made: direct materials
(d) royalty paid to designer: direct expenses
(e) salary of office assistant: indirect expenses*
(f) electricity used to heat the kilns: indirect expense (or possibly a direct expense – see note to question 4.6(d) above)
(g) rates of factory: indirect expense
(h) depreciation of office equipment: indirect expense
(i) wages of production line workers: direct labour
(j) salesperson's salary: indirect expenses*
(k) interest charged on bank overdraft: indirect expenses

* Note: Both the salary of the office assistant and the salesperson's salary have been classified as indirect expenses, rather than indirect labour. This is because neither of them work in the factory and so the cost cannot be attributed directly to production. By contrast, the wages of the factory supervisor are classified as indirect labour – here the employee does work in the factory, and the cost is more closely linked to production.

- *production overheads:* (a), (b), (f), (g)
- *selling and distribution overheads:* (j)
- *administration overheads:* (e), (h)
- *finance overheads:* (k)

4.9 **Task 1**

Dr **General Expenses Account** Cr

2007		£	2007		£
30 June	Balance b/d	28,250	30 June	Work-in-progress: treadmill	5,450
			30 June	Work-in-progress: exercise cycles	3,170
			30 June	Production overheads	12,950
			30 June	Non-production overheads: selling and distribution	3,860
			30 June	Non-production overheads: administration	2,820
		28,250			28,250

Task 2

2007	Code	Debit	Credit
30 June	2100	£5,450	
30 June	5150		£5,450
30 June	2200	£3,170	
30 June	5150		£3,170
30 June	3500	£12,950	
30 June	5150		£12,950
30 June	4200	£3,860	
30 June	5150		£3,860
30 June	4400	£2,820	
30 June	5150		£2,820

4.10 •

	high output	15,000 units	£65,000
less	low output	10,000 units	£50,000
equals	difference	5,000 units	£15,000

• amount of variable cost per unit:

$$\frac{£15,000}{5,000} = £3 \text{ variable cost per unit}$$

• at 10,000 units of output the cost structure is:

	total cost	£50,000
less	variable costs (10,000 units x £3 per unit)	£30,000
equals	fixed costs	£20,000

• check at 15,000 units of output when the cost structure is:

	variable costs (15,000 units x £3 per unit)	£45,000
add	fixed costs (as above)	£20,000
equals	total costs	£65,000

• therefore fixed costs, at these levels of output, are £20,000

4.11

2008	BUDGETED PRODUCTION COSTS		
Units	250,000	300,000	350,000
Costs	£	£	£
Variable costs:			
Materials	400,000	480,000	560,000
Labour	325,000	390,000	455,000
Expenses	100,000	120,000	140,000
	825,000	990,000	1,155,000
Fixed costs:			
Labour	96,500	96,500	96,500
Overheads	107,500	107,500	107,500
	204,000	204,000	204,000
TOTAL PRODUCTION COST	1,029,000	1,194,000	1,359,000
COST PER UNIT	£4.12	£3.98	£3.88

- Variable costs per unit are:
    - materials, £1.60 (ie £400,000 ÷ 250,000 units)
    - labour, £1.30
    - expenses, £0.40
- Fixed costs remain fixed at the higher levels of output
- The costs at higher levels of output are on the basis that
    - there is a linear relationship for variable costs
    - there are no stepped fixed costs
- The fall in cost per unit as output increases occurs because the fixed costs are being spread over a greater number of units, ie the fixed cost per unit falls

CHAPTER 5: OVERHEADS

5.1
- allocation of overheads – the charging to a cost centre of those overheads that have been directly incurred by that cost centre
- apportionment of overheads – the charging to a cost centre of a proportion of overheads

5.2 (a)

OVERHEAD ANALYSIS SHEET		
	MOULDING	FINISHING
Budgeted total overheads (£)	9,338	3,298
Budgeted machine hours	1,450	680
Budgeted overhead absorption rate (£)	6.44*	4.85**

*   £9,338 ÷ 1,450 hours

**   £3,298 ÷ 680 hours

(b)

JOB OVERHEAD ANALYSIS SHEET		
	MOULDING	FINISHING
Job machine hours	412	154
Budgeted overhead absorption rate (£)	6.44	4.85
Overhead absorbed by job (£)	2,653.28*	746.90**

*   412 hours x £6.44 per hour

**   154 hours x £4.85 per hour

(c) **Units of output**
- Using this method, production overhead is absorbed on the basis of each unit of output.
- This would be appropriate where units of output are identical and where each spend the

same amount of time in the departments.
- It does not seem appropriate for use by Wyvern Fabrication as the company appears to have different types and sizes of jobs passing through its two departments – to use units of output, each job would be charged the same rate.

Direct labour hour
- With this method, production overhead is absorbed on the basis of the number of direct labour hours worked.
- While this is a commonly-used method, it is inappropriate where some output is worked on by hand while other output passes quickly through a machinery process and requires little direct labour time.
- This method may be appropriate for Wyvern Fabrication; however, much depends on the balance between direct labour hours and machine hours in the two production departments.

5.3 (a)

cost	basis of apportionment	total	dept A	dept B	dept C
		£	£	£	£
Rent and rates	Floor area	7,210	3,090	1,545	2,575
Depn. of machinery	Value of machinery	10,800	5,400	3,240	2,160
Supervisor's salary	Production-line employees	12,750	6,800	3,400	2,550
Machinery insurance	Value of machinery	750	375	225	150
		31,510	15,665	8,410	7,435

(b) 37 hours x 48 weeks = 1,776 direct labour hours per employee
Dept A: 8 employees = 14,208 hours = £1.10 per direct labour hour
Dept B: 4 employees = 7,104 hours = £1.18 per direct labour hour
Dept C: 3 employees = 5,328 hours = £1.40 per direct labour hour

5.4 (a) and (b)

cost	basis of apportionment	total	machining	finishing	maintenance
		£	£	£	£
Rent and rates	Floor area	5,520	2,760	1,840	920
Buildings insurance	Floor area	1,320	660	440	220
Machinery insurance	Value of machinery	1,650	1,200	450	–
Lighting and heating	Floor area	3,720	1,860	1,240	620
Depn of machinery	Value of machinery	11,000	8,000	3,000	–
Supervisory salaries	No. of employees	30,000	18,000	9,000	3,000
Maintenance dept salary	Allocation	16,000	–	–	16,000
Factory cleaning	Floor area	4,800	2,400	1,600	800
		74,010	34,880	17,570	21,560
Re-apportionment of maintenance dept	Value of machinery	–	15,680	5,880	(21,560)
		74,010	50,560	23,450	–

(c)   35 hours x 47 weeks = 1,645 direct labour hours per employee
Machining Dept: 6 employees = 9,870 hours = £5.12 per direct labour hour
Finishing Dept: 3 employees = 4,935 hours = £4.75 per direct labour hour

(d)   Depending on the method and type of production, the company is most likely to use overhead absorption rates based on:
   •   direct labour hour, or
   •   machine hour
These are discussed in the text (pages 129 to 130). Alternative methods could be based on a percentage of certain costs, eg direct materials, direct labour, prime cost.

5.5

	total	business studies	general studies	administration	technical support
		£	£	£	£
Overheads	81,600	40,000	20,000	9,600	12,000
Technical support	–	6,000	3,000	3,000	(12,000)
				12,600	–
Administration	–	8,400	4,200	(12,600)	–
	81,600	54,400	27,200	–	–

5.6   (a) $\dfrac{\text{total overheads}}{\text{total hours}}$ $= \dfrac{£59,900}{3,290}$ $=$ £18.21 per partner hour

(b) $\dfrac{£59,900 + £60,000}{3,290}$ $=$ £36.44 per partner hour

(c)   2 hours x 47 weeks x £18.21 $=$ £1,711.74 per partner
(ie £3,423.48 in total)

5.7   (a)   Direct labour hour: (3 hours x 80 seats) + (3.5 hours x 40 seats)
= 380 direct labour hours per month = £2.63 per hour.

Machine hour: (1 hour x 80 seats) + (2.5 hours x 40 seats)
= 180 machine hours per month = £5.56 per hour.

Alternative methods could be based on a percentage of certain costs, eg direct labour.

(b)   *Direct labour hour*

'Standard'   £36.50 + £7.89   =   £44.39

'De Luxe'   £55.00 + £9.21   =   £64.21

Machine hour

'Standard'   £36.50 + £5.56   =   £42.06

'De Luxe'   £55.00 + £13.89   =   £68.89

Note: some figures have been rounded to the nearest penny

(c)   See text. The machine hour rate charges most to 'de luxe' model. On balance, direct labour hours may be the best method to use because the products are more labour-intensive than machine-intensive.

5.8 Task 1

Fixed overheads for November 2007	Basis	Total £	Warehouse £	Manufacturing £	Sales £	Administration £
Depreciation	Net book value	9,150	1,830	6,100	305	915
Rent	Floor space	11,000	1,650	6,600	1,100	1,650
Other property overheads	Floor space	6,200	930	3,720	620	930
Administration overheads	Allocated	13,450				13,450
Staff costs	Allocated	27,370	3,600	9,180	8,650	5,940
		67,170	8,010	25,600	10,675	22,885

Task 2

Budgeted fixed overhead absorption rate for the manufacturing department:

£25,600 ÷ 10,000 hours = £2.56 per machine hour

5.9 Task 1

Fixed overheads for August 2007	Basis	Total £	Accommodation £	Restaurant £	Bar £	Kitchen £	Administration £
Bedroom repairs	Allocated	3,200	3,200				
Electricity	Metered	1,700	550	250	150	700	50
Rent	Floor space	9,000	5,850	1,350	900	450	450
Kitchen repairs	Allocated	1,025				1,025	
Staff costs	Allocated	23,595	4,550	6,740	3,045	2,310	6,950
Other property overheads	Floor space	4,000	2,600	600	400	200	200
		42,520	16,750	8,940	4,495	4,685	7,650
Administration			4,590	1,530	765	765	(7,650)
		42,520	21,340	10,470	5,260	5,450	—

Task 2

Budgeted fixed overhead absorption rate for the kitchen:

£5,450 ÷ 1,000 hours = £5.45 per labour hour

5.10

Dr   **Production Overheads Account: Moulding Department**   Cr

	£		£
Bank (overheads incurred)	5,000	Work-in-progress	4,800
		Profit and loss (under-absorption)	200
	5,000		5,000

Dr   **Production Overheads Account: Finishing Department**   Cr

	£		£
Bank (overheads incurred)	7,000	Work-in-progress	7,500
Profit and loss (over-absorption)	500		
	7,500		7,500

2007	**Code**	**Debit**	**Credit**
26 May	3000	£4,800	
26 May	3400		£4,800
26 May	3000	£7,500	
26 May	3500		£7,500
26 May	6000	£200	
26 May	3400		£200
26 May	3500	£500	
26 May	6000		£500

CHAPTER 6: METHODS OF COSTING

6.1 The method of costing for each business should be justified; however, the following are the most likely methods:
- *accountant* – job costing, because each job will take a different length of time and is likely to involve a number of staff, each with different skill levels
- *bus company* – service costing, where the object is to find the cost per unit of service, eg passenger mile; job costing used for 'one-offs', eg quoting for the transport for a trip to the seaside for an old people's home
- *baker* – batch costing, where identical units are produced in batches, eg loaves; job costing could be used for 'one-off' items, eg a wedding cake
- *sports centre* – service costing, or job costing for 'one-off', eg hire of the main sports hall for an exhibition
- *hotel* – different methods of costing are likely to be used, eg service costing for the rooms, batch costing in the restaurant, and job costing for special events
- *construction company* – contract costing for large, complex projects which last for a long period of time; job costing for smaller, more routine work

6.2

			£	£
Direct materials:	100m x £7.50		750.00	
	75m x £4.00		300.00	
				1,050.00
Direct labour:	35 hours x £6.00			210.00
Overheads:	35 hours x £8.50			297.50
(a)	TOTAL COST			1,557.50
	Profit (20% of total cost)			311.50
(b)	SELLING PRICE			1,869.00

6.3

JOB COST SHEET
Replacement Cylinder Head

		£
Direct Materials		
100 kg of high-strength steel at £10 per kg		1,000.00
Direct Labour		
Foundry:	10 hours at £10.00 per hour	100.00
Finishing:	15 hours at £12.00 per hour	180.00
Overheads		
Foundry:	80% of direct labour cost	80.00
Finishing:	12 machine hours x £20 per hour	240.00
TOTAL COST		1,600.00
Profit (25% of total cost)		400.00
SELLING PRICE		2,000.00

6.4 *Total costs:*

	£
Depreciation of diesel trains £30,000* x 6 trains	180,000
Leasing charges for track	500,000
Maintenance charges for trains	455,000
Fuel for trains	105,000
Wages of drivers and conductors	240,000
Administration	260,000
	1,740,000

* (£650,000 – £50,000) ÷ 20 years = £30,000 per train per year

Cost per passenger mile:

$$\frac{£1,740,000}{2.5m\ journeys\ x\ 5\ miles} = £0.1392 \text{ per passenger mile}$$

6.5

Cost element	Costs	Completed Units	Work-in-progress			Total Equivalent Units	Cost per Unit	WIP valuation
			Units	% complete	Equivalent Units			
	A	B	C	D	E	F	G	H
					C x D	B + E	A ÷ F	E x G
	£						£	£
Direct materials	11,500	20,000	5,000	100	5,000	25,000	0.46	2,300
Direct labour	9,000	20,000	5,000	50	2,500	22,500	0.40	1,000
Production overheads	18,000	20,000	5,000	50	2,500	22,500	0.80	2,000
Total	38,500						1.66	5,300

(a)   Cost per toy is £1.66 each

(b)   Work-in-progress valuation is £5,300:

	£
20,000 completed units at £1.66 each	33,200
work-in-progress valuation	5,300
total costs for month	38,500

6.6

Dr   **Process Account**   Cr

	Quantity (litres)	Unit cost £	Total £		Quantity (litres)	Unit cost £	Total £
Materials	22,000	0.25	5,500	Normal loss			
Labour		0.15	3,300	(scrap sales)	2,000	–	400
Overheads		0.10	2,200	Finished goods	20,000	0.53	10,600
	22,000		11,000		22,000		11,000

Dr   **Normal Loss Account**   Cr

	£		£
Process account	400	Bank/debtors	400

Tutorial note:

The cost per unit of the expected output is:

$$\frac{£11,000 - £400}{20,000 \text{ litres}} = £0.53 \text{ per litre}$$

6.7

Dr   **Process Account**   Cr

	Quantity (kilos)	Unit cost £	Total £		Quantity (kilos)	Unit cost £	Total £
Materials	42,000	0.25	10,500	Normal loss	2,000	–	400
Labour		0.10	4,200	Finished goods	39,500	0.41	16,195
Overheads		0.05	2,100	Abnormal loss	500	0.41	205
	42,000		16,800		42,000		16,800

Dr   **Normal Loss Account**   Cr

	£		£
Process account	400	Bank/debtors	400

Dr   **Abnormal Loss Account**   Cr

	£		£
Process account	205	Bank/debtors (500 kilos x 20p)	100

Tutorial note:

The cost per unit of the expected output is:

$$\frac{£16,800 - £400}{40,000 \text{ kilos}} = £0.41 \text{ per kilo}$$

6.8

Dr   **Process 1 Account**   Cr

	Quantity (litres)	Unit cost £	Total £		Quantity (litres)	Unit cost £	Total £
Materials	10,000	0.50	5,000	Normal loss (10%)	1,000	–	400
Labour		0.40	4,000	Transfer to			
Overheads		0.20	2,000	process 2	9,000	1.18	10,600
	10,000		11,000		10,000		11,000

Dr   **Process 2 Account**   Cr

	Quantity (litres)	Unit cost £	Total £		Quantity (litres)	Unit cost £	Total £
Transfer from				Normal loss (5%)	450	–	225
process 1	9,000	1.18	10,600	Finished goods	8,300	1.58	13,130
Labour		0.20	1,800	Abnormal loss	250	1.58	395
Overheads		0.15	1,350				
	9,000		13,750		9,000		13,750

Dr   **Normal Loss Account**   Cr

	£		£
Process 1 account	400	Bank/debtors	400
Process 2 account	225	Bank/debtors	225
	625		625

Dr   **Abnormal Loss Account**   Cr

	£		£
Process 2 account	395	Bank/debtors (250 litres x 50p)	125

Tutorial notes:

- In process 1, the cost per unit of the expected output is:

$$\frac{£11,000 - £400}{9,000 \text{ litres}} = £1.18 \text{ per litre}$$

- In process 2, the cost per unit of the expected output is:

$$\frac{£13,750 - £225}{8,550 \text{ litres}} = £1.58 \text{ per litre}$$

6.9

Dr   **Process Account**   Cr

	Quantity (litres)	Unit cost £	Total £		Quantity (litres)	Unit cost £	Total £
Materials	11,000	0.50	5,500	Normal loss	1,000	–	300
Labour		0.35	3,850	Finished goods	10,200	1.18	12,036
Overheads		0.25	2,750				
			12,100				
Abnormal gain	200	1.18	236				
	11,200		12,336		11,200		12,336

Dr	**Abnormal Gain Account**		Cr
	£		£
Normal loss account	*60	Process account	236

Dr	**Normal Loss Account**		Cr
	£		£
Process account	300	Bank/debtors	240
		Abnormal gain account	*60
	300		300

* 200 litres at 30p per litre

Tutorial note:

The cost per unit of the expected output is:

$$\frac{£12,100 - £300}{10,000 \text{ litres}} = £1.18 \text{ per litre}$$

CHAPTER 7: BOOK-KEEPING FOR COSTING

7.1 (c)

7.2 (d)

7.3 (a) factory rent – manufacturing account

(b) production supervisors' wages – manufacturing account

(c) insurance of factory buildings – manufacturing account

(d) depreciation of office equipment – profit and loss account

(e) sales commission – profit and loss account

(f) raw materials purchased – manufacturing account

(g) advertising – profit and loss account

7.4

CROWN HEATH MANUFACTURING COMPANY
MANUFACTURING AND PROFIT AND LOSS ACCOUNT
for the year ended 31 December 2007

	£	£
Opening stock of raw materials		10,500
Add Purchases of raw materials		27,200
		37,700
Less Closing stock of raw materials		10,200
COST OF RAW MATERIALS USED		27,500
Direct labour		12,600
PRIME COST		40,100
Add Production overheads:		
Indirect labour	3,900	
Rent and rates	1,200	
Power	2,000	
Depreciation of factory machinery	900	
Repairs to factory buildings	300	
Sundry factory expenses	900	
		9,200
PRODUCTION COST OF GOODS COMPLETED		49,300
Sales		60,400
Opening stock of finished goods	4,300	
Production cost of goods completed	49,300	
	53,600	
Less Closing stock of finished goods	3,200	
COST OF SALES		50,400
Gross profit		10,000
Less Non-production overheads		6,500
Net profit		3,500

7.5

BARBARA FRANCIS
MANUFACTURING AND PROFIT AND LOSS ACCOUNT
for the year ended 31 December 2007

	£	£
Opening stock of raw materials		31,860
Add Purchases of raw materials		237,660
		269,520
Less Closing stock of raw materials		44,790
COST OF RAW MATERIALS USED		224,730
Direct labour		234,630
PRIME COST		459,360
Add Production overheads:		
Rent and rates	24,690	
Power	7,650	
Heat and light	2,370	
Sundry expenses and maintenance	8,190	
Depreciation of plant and machinery	7,450	
		50,350
PRODUCTION COST OF GOODS COMPLETED		509,710
Sales		796,950
Opening stock of finished goods	42,640	
Production cost of goods completed	509,710	
	552,350	
Less Closing stock of finished goods	96,510	
COST OF SALES		455,840
Gross profit		341,110
Less Non-production overheads:		
Rent and rates	8,230	
Salaries	138,700	
Advertising	22,170	
Office expenses	7,860	
		176,960
Net profit		164,150

7.6 *Note that transactions are recorded in the integrated book-keeping system in the order in which they took place.*

Dr		**Capital Account**		Cr
	£			£
Balance c/d	67,000	Bank		50,000
		Profit and loss		17,000
	67,000			67,000
		Balance b/d		67,000

Dr		**Bank Account**		Cr
	£			£
Capital	50,000	Machinery		20,000
Debtors	25,000	Labour		10,000
		Production overheads		5,000
		Non-production overheads		4,000
		Creditors		7,000
		Balance c/d		29,000
	75,000			75,000
Balance b/d	29,000			

Dr		**Machinery Account**		Cr
	£			£
Bank	20,000			

Dr		**Materials Account**		Cr
	£			£
Creditors	7,500	Work-in-progress		6,000
		Balance c/d		1,500
	7,500			7,500
Balance b/d	1,500			

Dr		**Creditors' Account**		Cr
	£			£
Bank	7,000	Materials		7,500
Balance c/d	500			
	7,500			7,500
		Balance b/d		500

Dr		Labour Costs Account		Cr
	£			£
Bank	10,000	Work-in-progress		10,000

Dr		Production Overheads Account		Cr
	£			£
Bank	5,000	Work-in-progress		5,000

Dr		Non-Production Overheads Account		Cr
	£			£
Bank	4,000	Profit and loss		4,000

Dr		Sales Account		Cr
	£			£
Profit and loss	37,000	Debtors		37,000

Dr		Debtors' Account		Cr
	£			£
Sales	37,000	Bank		25,000
		Balance c/d		12,000
	37,000			37,000
Balance b/d	12,000			

Dr		Work-in-Progress Account		Cr
	£			£
Direct materials	6,000	Finished goods		19,000
Direct labour	10,000	Balance c/d		2,000
Production overheads	5,000			
	21,000			21,000
Balance b/d	2,000			

Dr		Finished Goods Account		Cr
	£			£
Work-in-progress	19,000	Cost of sales		16,000
		Balance c/d		3,000
	19,000			19,000
Balance b/d	3,000			

Dr	**Cost of Sales Account**		Cr
	£		£
Finished goods	16,000	Profit and loss	16,000

Dr	**Profit and Loss Account**		Cr
	£		£
Non-production overheads	4,000	Sales	37,000
Cost of sales	16,000		
Net profit (to Capital account)	17,000		
	37,000		37,000

Trial balance at 31 July 2007

	Dr	Cr
	£	£
Capital		67,000
Bank	29,000	
Machinery	20,000	
Materials	1,500	
Creditors		500
Debtors	12,000	
Work-in-progress	2,000	
Finished goods	3,000	
	67,500	67,500

7.7 • work-in-progress account £16,500: the cost of direct labour incurred by the company for the week on manufacturing the product

• production overheads accounts £5,900: the cost of indirect labour incurred by the company for the week

7.8 • Debit: profit and loss account £125

• Credit: production overheads account £125

The amount of under-absorbed overhead is debited to profit and loss account where it adds to the total costs of the business, and so reduces profit.

7.9 • Debit: production overheads account (finishing department)

• Credit: profit and loss account

The amount of over-absorbed overhead is credited to profit and loss account where it increases profit.

7.10 **Department A**

- overhead absorbed by cost units £3.00 x 1,240 hours   =   £3,720
- actual cost of production overhead   =   £3,800
- under-absorption of overhead   =   £   80

Department B

- overhead absorbed by cost units £6.00 x 1,660 hours   =   £9,960
- actual cost of production overhead   =   £9,040
- over-absorption of overhead   =   £ 920

Dr	**Production Overheads Account: Department A**		Cr
	£		£
Bank (overheads incurred)	3,800	Work-in-progress	3,720
		Profit and loss (under-absorption)	80
	3,800		3,800

Dr	**Production Overheads Account: Department B**		Cr
	£		£
Bank (overheads incurred)	9,040	Work-in-progress	9,960
Profit and loss (over-absorption)	920		
	9,960		9,960

7.11

Dr				**Process Account**				Cr
	Quantity (litres)	Unit cost £	Total £		Quantity (litres)	Unit cost £	Total £
Materials	22,000	0.70	15,400	Normal loss	1,800	–	900
Labour			6,600	Finished goods	20,300	1.25	25,375
Overheads			4,150				
			26,150				
Abnormal gain	100	1.25	125				
	22,100		26,275		22,100		26,275

Dr		Abnormal Gain Account			Cr
		£			£
Normal loss account		*50	Process account		125

Dr		Normal Loss Account			Cr
		£			£
Process account		900	Bank/debtors		850
			Abnormal gain account		*50
		900			900

* 100 litres at 50p per litre

Tutorial note:

The cost per unit of the expected output is:

$$\frac{£26,150 - £900}{20,200 \text{ litres}} = £1.25 \text{ per litre}$$

7.12

Dr			Process 1 Account				Cr
	Quantity	Unit cost	Total		Quantity	Unit cost	Total
	(kilos)	£	£		(kilos)	£	£
Materials	4,000	3.00	12,000	Normal loss (10%)	400	–	200
Labour			1,840	Transfer to			
Overheads			2,150	process 2	3,700	4.39	16,229
			15,990				
Abnormal gain	100	4.39	439				
	4,100		16,429		4,100		16,429

Dr			Process 2 Account				Cr
	Quantity	Unit cost	Total		Quantity	Unit cost	Total
	(kilos)	£	£		(kilos)	£	£
Transfer from				Normal loss (20%)	1,180	–	590
process 1	3,700	4.39	16,229	Finished goods	4,600	5.70	26,225
Materials	2,200	4.00	8,800	Abnormal loss	120	5.70	684
Labour			1,420				
Overheads			1,050				
	5,900		27,499		5,900		27,499

Dr		**Normal Loss Account**	Cr
	£		£
Process 1 account	200	Bank/debtors	150
Process 2 account	590	Abnormal gain account	*50
		Bank/debtors	590
	790		790

Dr		**Abnormal Gain Account**	Cr
	£		£
Normal loss account	*50	Process 1 account	439

* 100 kilos at £0.50 per kilo

Dr		**Abnormal Loss Account**	Cr
	£		£
Process 2 account	684	Bank/debtors (120 kilos x £0.50)	60

Tutorial notes:

- In process 1, the cost per unit of the expected output is:

  $$\frac{£15,990 - £200}{3,600 \text{ kilos}} = £4.39 \text{ per kilo}$$

- In process 2, the cost per unit of the expected output is:

  $$\frac{£27,499 - £590}{4,720 \text{ kilos}} = £5.70 \text{ per kilo}$$

- At the end of the financial year:
  - the balance of abnormal loss account is debited to profit and loss account
  - the balance of abnormal gain account is credited to profit and loss account

CHAPTER 8: SHORT-TERM DECISIONS

8.1

units of output	fixed costs	variable costs	total cost	sales revenue	profit/(loss)*
	£	£	£	£	£
0	7,500	0	7,500	0	(7,500)
500	7,500	2,500	10,000	5,000	(5,000)
1,000	7,500	5,000	12,500	10,000	(2,500)
1,500	7,500	7,500	15,000	15,000	nil
2,000	7,500	10,000	17,500	20,000	2,500
2,500	7,500	12,500	20,000	25,000	5,000
3,000	7,500	15,000	22,500	30,000	7,500

* brackets indicate a loss

8.2 Graphical method

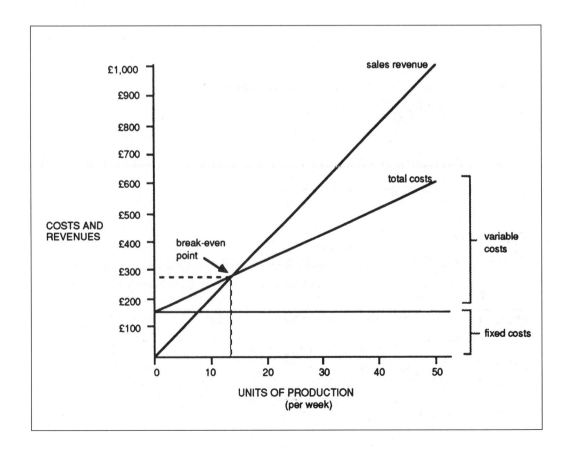

Calculation method

The contribution per unit is:

		£
	selling price per unit	20
less	variable costs* per unit	9
equals	contribution per unit	11

* materials £4 + direct labour £5

The break-even calculation is:

$$\frac{\text{fixed costs (£)}}{\text{contribution per unit (£)}} = \frac{£154^{**}}{£11} = 14 \text{ units (teddy bears) per week}$$

** factory rent and rates £100 + fuel and power £20 + other costs £20

8.3   (a)   table method

units of output	fixed costs	variable costs	total cost	sales revenue	profit/(loss)*
	£	£	£	£	£
100	12,000	2,000	14,000	3,500	(10,500)
200	12,000	4,000	16,000	7,000	(9,000)
300	12,000	6,000	18,000	10,500	(7,500)
400	12,000	8,000	20,000	14,000	(6,000)
500	12,000	10,000	22,000	17,500	(4,500)
600	12,000	12,000	24,000	21,000	(3,000)
700	12,000	14,000	26,000	24,500	(1,500)
800	12,000	16,000	28,000	28,000	nil
900	12,000	18,000	30,000	31,500	1,500
1,000	12,000	20,000	32,000	35,000	3,000
1,100	12,000	22,000	34,000	38,500	4,500
1,200	12,000	24,000	36,000	42,000	6,000

* brackets indicate a loss

(b) **graph method**

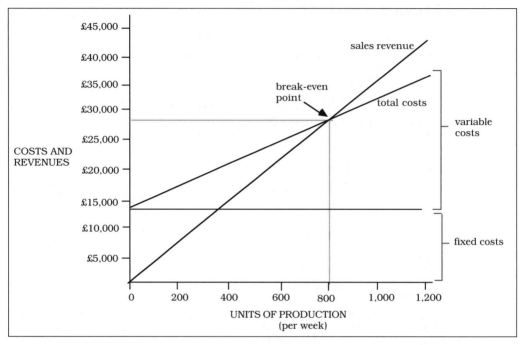

(c) **calculation method**

Fixed costs of £12,000 ÷ contribution of £15 per bat = 800 bats to break-even.

(d) **profit/(loss)**

• 200 bats

	£
Sales (£35 per bat)	7,000
Less variable costs (£20 per bat)	4,000
Contribution	3,000
Less fixed costs	12,000
Loss for month	(9,000)

• 1,200 bats

	£
Sales (£35 per bat)	42,000
Less variable costs (£20 per bat)	24,000
Contribution	18,000
Less fixed costs	12,000
Profit for month	6,000

(e) **margin of safety**

$$\frac{\text{current output} - \text{break-even output}}{\text{current output}} \times \frac{100}{1} = \frac{1,000 - 800}{1,000}$$

= 20 per cent, or 200 units

8.4 **Task 1**

- profit volume ratio

$$\frac{\text{contribution (£)}}{\text{selling price (£)}} \quad = \frac{£15^*}{£25} \quad = \ 0.6 \text{ or } 60\%$$

  * selling price £25 – variable cost £10

- break-even point in units

$$\frac{\text{fixed costs (£)}}{\text{contribution per unit (£)}} \quad = \frac{£300,000}{£15} = \ 20,000 \text{ units}$$

- break-even point in sales revenue

$$\frac{\text{fixed costs (£)}}{\text{PV ratio}} \quad = \frac{£300,000}{0.6} = \ £500,000$$

  check: 20,000 units x selling price £25 per unit = £500,000

- margin of safety at output of 30,000 units

$$\frac{\text{current output – break-even output}}{\text{current output}} \ = \ \frac{30,000 - 20,000}{30,000} \ \text{x} \ \frac{100}{1}$$

  = 33.3%, or 10,000 units, or £250,000 of sales revenue

- number of units to generate a target profit of £100,000

$$\frac{\text{fixed costs (£) + target profit (£)}}{\text{contribution per unit (£)}} \quad = \quad \frac{£300,000 + £100,000}{£15} \ = 26,667 \text{ units}$$

Task 2

		forecast output (30,000 units)	maximum output (40,000 units)
		£	£
	sales revenue (at £25 each)	750,000	1,000,000
less	variable costs (at £10 each)	300,000	400,000
equals	contribution (to fixed costs and profit)	450,000	600,000
less	monthly fixed costs	300,000	300,000
equals	forecast profit for month	150,000	300,000

Task 3

- profit volume ratio

  $$\frac{£10^*}{£20} \quad = \quad 0.5 \text{ or } 50\%$$

  * selling price £20 – variable cost £10

- break-even point in units

  $$\frac{£300,000}{£10} \quad = \quad 30,000 \text{ units}$$

- break-even point in sales revenue

  $$\frac{£300,000}{0.5} \quad = \quad £600,000$$

  check: 30,000 units x selling price £20 per unit = £600,000

- margin of safety at maximum output of 40,000 units

  $$\frac{40,000 - 30,000}{40,000} \text{ x } \frac{100}{1} \quad = 25\%, \text{ or } 10,000 \text{ units, or } £200,000 \text{ of sales revenue}$$

- forecast profit at sales of 40,000 units

		£
	sales revenue (at £20 each)	800,000
less	variable costs (at £10 each)	400,000
equals	contribution (to fixed costs and profit)	400,000
less	monthly fixed costs	300,000
equals	forecast profit for month	100,000

REPORT

To: General Manager

From: Accounts Assistant

Date: Today

Proposal to reduce selling price

Introduction

- You asked me to report on the suggestion from one of the managers that the selling price for our product should be reduced from £25 per unit to £20.

Workings (using figures for July):

- direct materials per meal = £25,125 ÷ 33,500 meals = £0.75

- direct labour per meal = £15,075 ÷ 33,500 meals = £0.45

- direct expenses per meal = £6,700 ÷ 33,500 meals = £0.20

- overheads for Indian meals production line

	meals	£
high	34,700	12,705
low	31,000	12,150
difference	3,700	555

variable cost per meal = £555 ÷ 3,700 meals = £0.15

fixed cost = £12,525 – (£0.15 x 33,500 meals) = £7,500

- other production overheads: fixed cost = £4,000 per month

- sales revenue per meal = £67,000 ÷ 33,500 meals = £2.00

Task 2

DURNING FOODS LIMITED: Production line for Indian meals

Planned results for November 2007: increased activity

Number of meals to be sold	40,000
	£
Direct materials at 75p – 20% = 60p per meal	24,000
Direct labour at 45p per meal	18,000
Direct expenses at 20p per meal	8,000
Overheads for Indian meals production line at £7,500 + 15p per meal	13,500
Other production overheads	4,000
Total cost	67,500
Sales revenue at £2.00 per meal	80,000
Profit	12,500

Break-even point

		£	£
Contribution per meal:			
	selling price		2.00
less	variable costs:		
	direct materials	0.60	
	direct labour	0.45	
	direct expenses	0.20	
	production line overheads	0.15	
			1.40
equals	contribution per meal		0.60
Fixed costs:			
	production line overheads		7,500
	other production overheads		4,000
			11,500

Break-even point:

$$\frac{£11,500}{£0.60} = 19,167 \text{ meals}$$

Margin of safety

$$\frac{40,000 - 19,167}{40,000} \times \frac{100}{1} = 52\%$$

8.8 The marginal cost per unit of Exe is £5 (direct materials £3 + direct labour £2), and so any contribution, ie selling price less marginal cost, will be profit:

• *200 units at £6 each*

The offer price of £6 is above the marginal cost of £5 and increases profit by the amount of the £1 extra contribution, ie (£6 – £5) x 200 units = £200 extra profit.

• *500 units at £4 each*

This offer price is below the marginal cost of £5; therefore there will be a fall in profit if this order is undertaken of (£4 – £5) x 500 units = £500 reduced profit.

WESTFIELD LIMITED
monthly profit statements

	Existing production of 2,000 units £	Existing production + 200 units @ £6 each £	Existing production + 500 units @ £4 each £
Sales revenue (per month):			
2,000 units at £12 each	24,000	24,000	24,000
200 units at £6 each	–	1,200	–
500 units at £4 each	–	–	2,000
	24,000	25,200	26,000
Less production costs:			
Direct materials (£3 per unit)	6,000	6,600	7,500
Direct labour (£2 per unit)	4,000	4,400	5,000
Production overheads (fixed)	8,000	8,000	8,000
PROFIT	6,000	6,200	5,500

The conclusion is that the first special order should be accepted, and the second declined.

8.9

POPCAN LIMITED
monthly profit statements

	Existing production of 150,000 cans £	Existing production + 50,000 cans at 18p each £
Sales revenue (per month):		
150,000 cans at 25p each	37,500	37,500
50,000 cans at 18p each	–	9,000
	37,500	46,500
Less production costs:		
Direct materials (5p per can)	7,500	10,000
Direct labour (5p per can)	7,500	10,000
Production overheads – variable (4p per can)	6,000	8,000
– fixed*	9,000	9,000
PROFIT	7,500	9,500

* 6p x 150,000 cans = £9,000

The offer from the supermarket chain should be accepted because:

- the marginal cost of producing each can is 14p (direct materials 5p, direct labour 5p, variable production overheads 4p)

- the offer price is 18p per can, which is above marginal cost, and gives a contribution of 4p

- profits increase by the amount of the extra contribution, ie (18p – 14p) x 50,000 cans = £2,000 extra profit

8.10

MAXXA LIMITED
Profit statement for the month ended 31 January 2007

	MARGINAL COSTING		ABSORPTION COSTING	
	£	£	£	£
Sales 3,000 units at £8 each		24,000		24,000
Variable costs				
Direct materials at £1.25 each	5,000		5,000	
Direct labour at £2.25 each	9,000		9,000	
	14,000			
Less Closing stock (marginal cost)				
1,000 units at £3.50 each	3,500			
	10,500			
Fixed production overheads	6,000		6,000	
			20,000	
Less Closing stock (absorption cost)				
1,000 units at £5 each			5,000	
Less Cost of goods sold		16,500		15,000
PROFIT		7,500		9,000

Working notes:

Closing stock is calculated on the basis of this year's costs:

marginal costing, variable costs only, ie £1.25 + £2.25 = £3.50 per unit

absorption costing, variable and fixed costs, ie £20,000 ÷ 4,000 units = £5 per unit

The difference in the profit is caused only by the closing stock figures: £3,500 under marginal costing, and £5,000 under absorption costing. With marginal costing, the full amount of the fixed production overheads has been charged in this year's profit statement; by contrast, with absorption costing, part of the fixed production overheads (here £6,000 x 25%* = £1,500) has been carried forward in the stock valuation.

* 1,000 units in stock out of 4,000 units manufactured

CHAPTER 9: LONG-TERM DECISIONS

9.1 (a) payback period

	PROJECT EXE			PROJECT WYE	
Year	Cash Flow	Cumulative Cash Flow		Cash Flow	Cumulative Cash Flow
	£000	£000		£000	£000
0	(80)	(80)		(100)	(100)
1	40	(40)		20	(80)
2	40	–		30	(50)
3	20	20		50	–
4	10	30		50	50
5	10	40		40	90

As can be seen from the above table:

- Project Exe pays back after two years
- Project Wye pays back after three years

(b) net present value

		PROJECT EXE			PROJECT WYE	
Year	Discount Factor	Cash Flow £000	Discounted Cash Flow £000		Cash Flow £000	Discounted Cash Flow £000
0	1.000	(80)	(80)		(100)	(100)
1	0.893	40	35.72		20	17.86
2	0.797	40	31.88		30	23.91
3	0.712	20	14.24		50	35.60
4	0.636	10	6.36		50	31.80
5	0.567	10	5.67		40	22.68
Net Present Value (NPV)			13.87			31.85

REPORT

To:	Robert Smith
From:	Accounts Assistant
Date:	Today

Capital investment projects: Exe and Wye

I have carried out an appraisal of these two projects, based on the information provided. I have used two techniques:

• payback

• net present value

The first of these, payback, sees how long it takes for the initial outlay of the project to be repaid by the net cash flow coming in. For Project Exe, the payback period is two years; for Project Wye, it is three years. Using this technique, Project Exe is more favourable.

Payback is an easy technique both to calculate and understand. However, it does have the disadvantage of ignoring all cash flows after the payback period. With these two projects, Wye has strong cash inflows in years 4 and 5, after the payback period (however, these could be a disadvantage if the project is likely to go out-of-date soon).

The net present value (NPV) technique relies on discounting relevant cash flows at an appropriate rate of return, which is 12 per cent for these projects. Net present value is a more sophisticated technique than payback in that it uses all cash flows and takes the timing of cash flows into account. However, the meaning of NPV is not always clear, and the rate of return required on the projects may vary over their life.

Project Wye has a higher NPV (but also a higher initial cost) at £31,850, when compared with Exe at £13,870. The fact that both figures are positive means that either project will be worthwhile. However, in view of the differing initial costs, it would be appropriate to calculate the Internal rate of return, so that a comparison can be made directly between the two projects.

9.2 **Task 1**

The net cash flows are:

	£000
year 1	(95)
year 2	30
year 3	40
year 4	50
year 5	25

(a)   payback period

Year	Cash Flow	Cumulative Cash Flow	
	£000	£000	
1	(95)	(95)	
2	30	(65)	
3	40	(25)	
4	50	25	∴ £25,000 required
5	25	50	

The design costs are recovered half-way through year 4: £30,000 + £40,000 + (£25,000/£50,000 x 12 months). Thus the payback period is 3 years and 6 months from the start of the project; in terms of revenue, the payback period is 2 years and 6 months. Note that these assume even cash flows during the year.

(b)   net present value

Year	Cash Flow		Discount Factor	Discounted Cash Flow
	£000			£000
1	(95)	x	0.909	(86.35)
2	30	x	0.826	24.78
3	40	x	0.751	30.04
4	50	x	0.683	34.15
5	25	x	0.621	15.52
			Net Present Value (NPV)	18.14

Task 2

- For this new project IRR, at almost 20 per cent, is much higher than the 10% return required on new projects.

- This means that, in financial terms, the new project is acceptable – the wider the margin of IRR above the return required, the better.

9.3 Task 1

DURNING FOODS LIMITED

Working paper for the financial appraisal of purchase of delivery vehicles

DISCOUNTED CASH FLOW

Year	Cash Flow	Discount Factor at 12%	Discounted Cash Flow
	£		£
2007	(80,000)	1.000	(80,000)
2008	28,300	0.893	25,272
2009	28,300	0.797	22,555
2010	28,300	0.712	20,150
2011	*38,300	0.636	24,359
Net Present Value (NPV)			12,336

* £28,300 + £10,000 resale value

PAYBACK PERIOD

Year	Cash Flow	Cumulative Cash Flow	
	£	£	
2007	(80,000)	(80,000)	
2008	28,300	(51,700)	
2009	28,300	(23,400)	
2010	28,300	4,900	£23,400* required
2011	38,300	43,200	

* £28,300 – £4,900

Payback period =   2 years + (£23,400/£28,300) = 2.8 years, ie 2 years and 10 months

Task 2

REPORT
To: General Manager **From:**   Accounts Assistant **Date:**   12 November 2007
 Purchase of delivery vehicles The proposal to purchase delivery vehicles is acceptable from a financial viewpoint because it returns a positive net present value of £12,336 at a discount rate of 12 per cent. This calculation assumes that all cash flows occur at the end of each year. The payback period is during 2010. If we assume even cash flows during the year, the payback period can be calculated as 2.8 years (or 2 years and 10 months) from the start. This is acceptable since it is shorter than the company requirement of three years, although there is not a great deal of room for error in the cash flow calculations.

9.4   Task 1

The net cash flows are:

	£000
year 0	(40)
year 1	(60)
year 2	45
year 3	54
year 4	90
year 5	60

(a)   payback period

Year	Cash Flow	Cumulative Cash Flow	
	£000	£000	
0	(40)	(40)	
1	(60)	(100)	
2	45	(55)	
3	54	(1)	
4	90	89	∴ £1,000 required
5	60	149	

The development costs are recovered in the very early part of year 4: £45,000 + £54,000 + (£1,000/£90,000 x 12 months). Thus the payback period is 3 years and 0.13 months (ie less than one week into the next year) from the start of the project; in terms of revenue, the payback period is 2 years and 0.13 months. Note that these assume even cash flows during the year.

(b)   net present value

Year	Cash Flow		Discount Factor	Discounted Cash Flow
	£000			£000
0	(40)	x	1.000	(40)
1	(60)	x	0.893	(53.58)
2	45	x	0.797	35.86
3	54	x	0.712	38.45
4	90	x	0.636	57.24
5	60	x	0.567	34.02
			Net Present Value (NPV)	71.99

Task 2

REPORT

To: Managing Director

From: Accounts Assistant

Date: Today

Introduction of a new range of bikes

I have carried out an appraisal on the project, based on the information provided.

The net present value technique relies on discounting relevant cash flows at an appropriate rate of return. It would be helpful to know:

1.   whether there are any additional cash flows beyond year 5

2.   whether the introduction of a new range of bikes will affect sales of our existing bikes

On the basis of the information provided, the project has a positive net present value of £71,990 and should be carried out.

9.5 numerical assessments using net present value methods

Year	Cash Flow		Discount Factor		Discounted Cash Flow
	£				£
Outright purchase					
0	(10,000)	x	1.000	=	(10,000)
5	1,000	x	0.621	=	621
			Net Present Value (NPV)	=	(9,379)
Hire purchase					
0	(4,000)	x	1.000	=	(4,000)
1	(4,000)	x	0.909	=	(3,636)
2	(4,000)	x	0.826	=	(3,304)
5	1,000	x	0.621	=	621
			Net Present Value (NPV)	=	(10,319)
Leasing					
1	(2,500)	x	0.909	=	(2,272.50)
2	(2,500)	x	0.826	=	(2,065.00)
3	(2,500)	x	0.751	=	(1,877.50)
4	(2,500)	x	0.683	=	(1,707.50)
5	(2,500)	x	0.621	=	(1,552.50)
			Net Present Value (NPV)	=	(9,475.00)

Tutorial note: We are using NPV here with <u>costs</u>: therefore the best project (in financial terms) has the <u>lowest</u> NPV, which is the least cost to the business.

advice to Ken Jones

- Outright purchase is marginally more attrractive than leasing the equipment.

- Hire purchase ranks third.

- Much depends on the financial position of your business – although outright purchase comes out the best, you will have to have the cash to pay for the equipment at the beginning.

- On balance, leasing may be the most suitable option for you, with regular annual payments being made over the period you plan to use the equipment.

Appendix
Photocopiable documents

STOCK RECORD

Stock description ....

Stock units ....

Stock ref. No. ....

Location ....

Minimum ....

Maximum ....

Re-order level ....

Re-order quantity ....

DATE	GOODS RECEIVED		GOODS ISSUED		BALANCE
	Reference	Quantity	Reference	Quantity	

STOCK RECORD

Stock description ....

Stock units ....

Stock ref. No. ....

Location ....

Minimum ....

Maximum ....

Re-order level ....

Re-order quantity ....

DATE	GOODS RECEIVED		GOODS ISSUED		BALANCE
	Reference	Quantity	Reference	Quantity	

STORES LEDGER RECORD

Date	Receipts			Issues			Balance		
	Quantity	Cost	Total Cost	Quantity	Cost	Total Cost	Quantity	Cost	Total Cost
		£	£		£	£		£	£

REPORT/MEMORANDUM
To:
From:
Date:

Index